WELCOME

To the story of the boy who would become king. Born to Britain's longest-reigning sovereign, the future King Charles III endured many years of hardship and heartache, from his difficult school days to his turbulent marriage to Diana, the Princess of Wales, and the many challenges of raising two sons in the glare of the public spotlight. Yet he has also enjoyed many highs, from his relationship with Camilla to his efforts to battle climate change and his enduring bond with a public who now call him their king. Turn the page to embark on his journey from a sensitive young boy to a dutiful modern monarch.

CONTENTS

6 **The House of Windsor**
Chart the growth of the British royal family, from Queen Elizabeth II and her husband Philip to King Charles III, Prince William and his three heirs

36 **Cadet to commander**
Charles's time in the forces proved to be a hectic and often stressful period of national duty

EARLY LIFE

10 **An enduring love**
Scarred by the trauma of World War II, Britain was helped to heal by the love of its future queen and the man who would always stand beside her

16 **The prince of hope**
The birth of Prince Charles in November 1948 secured the royal line and gave the nation a new reason to celebrate

22 **The prince in turmoil**
What should have been a happy time spent learning and making new friends at school turned into a period of anguish for Charles

30 **The investiture of a prince**
Charles would be forced to confront the threat of paramilitaries on the day that he was formally recognised as the Prince of Wales

LOVE

42 **Sowing his wild oats**
Once the most coveted bachelor on the planet, the future king enjoyed the company of several potential suitors before meeting Diana

52 **Prince Charles & Diana Spencer**
The marriage of Charles and a pretty young nanny gave Britain a real-life fairytale to celebrate

58 **A prince is born**
The arrival of Prince William in the summer of 1982 provided Charles with an heir and was met with widespread joy by the country

64 **Hurrah for Harry**
Despite the birth of their second son, Charles and Diana's marriage was slowly eroding

68 **On the rocks**
Straining to keep up appearances, behind the scenes Charles and Diana's marriage was floundering

72 The end of a fairytale
Amid a storm of salacious headlines, the couple's marriage finally came to an end in 1992

HEARTACHE & HAPPINESS

80 Death of a princess
A horrendous car crash in the heart of Paris claimed the lives of three people, including the woman hailed as 'the people's princess', and sent Britain into a period of stunned mourning

88 Single parent
Helping his sons to heal in the wake of their mother's death was a delicate process for Charles

94 Rekindling true love
Two former lovers gave new life to an old flame when Charles and Camilla made their relationship public, but many struggled to forgive their affair so soon after Diana's death

98 The wedding of Charles & Camilla
Inside the wedding that finally joined two kindred spirits in matrimony

LEGACY

102 Sport & culture
Being a modern royal means a busy schedule, but King Charles III has always been sure to carve out time to pursue his own interests

106 Living in the spotlight
No family on Earth is as scrutinised as the British royal family, and at times King Charles III has clashed with the media

110 A family duty
Ever conscious of the opportunities and access his status affords him, King Charles III has worked to bring people together in support of various causes close to his heart

118 Dedicated to sustainability
A vocal proponent of green policies and environmental protections long before the current climate crisis, Britain's new king has never been shy when it comes to voicing his opinion on key social matters

124 Long live the king
The devastating announcement of Queen Elizabeth II's death in September 2022 plunged a family and a nation into mourning, but as the world paid its respects protocol demanded that a grieving son must prepare to ascend the throne

 Order of succession
 Marriage
 Divorced

THE HOUSE OF WINDSOR

Founded in 1917, five members of the House of Windsor have reigned as the nation's monarch to date, and with William and Kate now the parents of three children, the future of the royal family is well secured

2

CAMILLA, QUEEN CONSORT
1947-NOW

Since marrying Charles, Camilla has embraced her role and become an active patron for several charities.

KING CHARLES III
1948-NOW
2022-NOW

After his divorce from Diana, Charles rekindled his relationship with Camilla. The two married in 2005.

DIANA, PRINCESS OF WALES
1961-1997

After her divorce, Diana continued to promote charities. Her untimely death in 1997 plunged the nation into a state of mourning.

TIMOTHY LAURENCE
1955-NOW

Now a retired Royal Navy officer, Timothy met Anne while serving as the Queen's equerry in 1986. They married in 1992.

PRINCESS ANNE
1950-NOW

Anne is largely championed as the hardest-working member of the royal family alongside her elder brother.

3

WILLIAM
1982-NOW

When William and Catherine married the two were bestowed the title of Duke and Duchess of Cambridge.

CATHERINE
1982-NOW

Catherine and William met at university and dated for several years before marrying in Westminster Abbey in April 2011.

HARRY
1984-NOW

Since his marriage to Meghan Markle in May 2018, Harry was given the title of Duke of Sussex and Meghan the Duchess.

MEGHAN
1981-NOW

Meghan and Harry's relationship has often caused a stir. In January 2020 the couple declared they were "stepping back" from their roles as senior royals.

4

GEORGE	CHARLOTTE	LOUIS	ARCHIE	LILIBET
2013-NOW	2015-NOW	2018-NOW	2019-NOW	2021-NOW

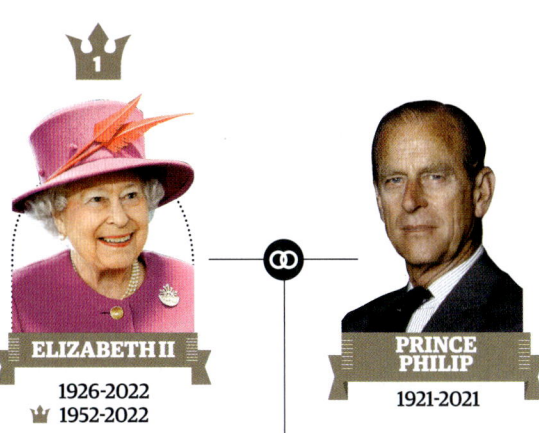

ELIZABETH II
1926-2022
👑 1952-2022

PRINCE PHILIP
1921-2021

Now both fathers, William and Harry have secured the Windsor lineage for many decades to come

MARK PHILLIPS
1948-NOW

Mark and Anne married in 1973 and divorced in 1992. Mark won an Olympic Gold medal in 1972 in the equestrian events.

ANDREW, DUKE OF YORK
1960-NOW

The third child of the Queen, Andrew has garnered much media coverage through various scandals, as well as his divorce.

SARAH FERGUSON
1959-NOW

Sarah and Andrew married in 1986 and divorced in 1996. Sarah was friends with Diana before and during their marriages.

EDWARD, EARL OF WESSEX
1964-NOW

The Queen's youngest son works as a member of the royal family full time and chose to become an earl after marriage.

SOPHIE, COUNTESS OF WESSEX
1965-NOW

Sophie and Edward married in 1999. Before marrying into the royal family Sophie worked as a PR executive.

PETER
1977-NOW

The first of the Queen's grandchildren, Peter married Autumn Kelly in 2008 and they had two children. In February 2020 they announced their separation.

ZARA
1981-NOW

An award-winning equestrian and Olympian, Zara married rugby player Mike Tindall and the couple have three children together.

BEATRICE
1988-NOW

Beatrice is a popular member of the royal family. She married property developer Edoardo Mapelli Mozzi in 2020, and the couple welcomed their first child, daughter Sienna, in 2021.

EUGENIE
1990-NOW

Princess Eugenie works at a London art gallery and does not carry out official engagements. She married Jack Brooksbank in October 2018, with whom she has a son.

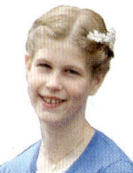

LOUISE
2003-NOW

Known as Lady Louise Windsor, unlike her cousins she is not a HRH. She was a bridesmaid at Prince William's wedding in 2011.

JAMES
2007-NOW

Like his sister, James in not a HRH and is instead known as James, Viscount Severn.

EARLY LIFE

10 **An enduring love**
Scarred by the trauma of WWII, Britain was helped to heal by the love of its future queen and the man who always stood beside her

16 **The prince of hope**
The birth of Prince Charles in November 1948 secured the royal line and gave the nation a new reason to celebrate

22 **The prince in turmoil**
What should have been a happy time spent learning and making new friends at school turned into a period of anguish for Charles

30 **The investiture of a prince**
Charles would be forced to confront the threat of paramilitaries on the day that he was formally recognised as the Prince of Wales

36 **Cadet to commander**
Charles's time in the forces proved to be a hectic and often stressful period of national duty

The young couple looked very much in love on their wedding day

AN ENDURING LOVE

As Britain recovered from the horrors of World War II it basked in the romantic love story of Princess Elizabeth and Prince Philip

Words **Jessica Leggett**

For over seven decades Queen Elizabeth and Prince Philip were the foundation of the British monarchy. The story of their relationship, from a young romance to their marriage, endeared them to the public at a time when the majority of royals married for duty rather than for love. Their wedding came at a time when the people of Britain, weary from the war, craved a distraction, and it became one of the most-celebrated events of the 20th century.

Princess Elizabeth was just eight years old when she first set eyes on her third cousin, Prince Philip, at the wedding of Princess Marina of Greece and Denmark to Prince George, Duke of Kent, in 1934. Five years later they would meet again, at the Royal Naval College in Dartmouth in July 1939. This time Elizabeth, now 13 years old, fell head over heels in love with Philip, who had turned into a handsome 18-year-old man.

The pair managed to spend a lot of time together that day, as Philip's uncle, Lord Louis Mountbatten, had arranged for his nephew to chaperone both the princess and her sister, Princess Margaret. After connecting at the college, Elizabeth and Philip agreed to exchange letters while they were apart, and soon enough the princess started to keep a framed photo of her beloved by her bed.

With the outbreak of World War II just months later, Elizabeth and Philip found themselves separated over the next six years, just like millions of other couples across the country. While Philip served in the British Royal Navy, the princess trained as a driver and mechanic, working for the Auxiliary Territorial Service in 1945. Elizabeth and Philip remained in contact during these harrowing times, with the latter even making a brief visit to Windsor to watch the princess perform in a pantomime with her sister.

When the war finally ended in 1945 there was a sigh of relief across Great Britain. Elizabeth and Philip were still in love, and it became obvious to onlookers that their romance was indeed serious. Elizabeth's father, King George VI, invited Philip to Balmoral in 1946. It was during this visit that the prince took the plunge and asked Elizabeth to marry him, after seeking permission from her father. George consented, but on the condition that the engagement remain a secret until Elizabeth's 21st birthday in April 1947.

However, this was not just about giving Elizabeth time to consider her decision. Her father, along with the rest of the royal family, were concerned that Philip was not a suitable choice for the husband of the future queen. There were no advantages to be made from a marriage between the two - although Philip was a prince, he was practically penniless, and his family had been exiled from Greece after the abdication of his uncle, King Constantine I.

In addition to this, Elizabeth's family were well aware of the chaotic situation surrounding Philip's parents. While Elizabeth had a close and loving upbringing, Philip was left alone to be raised in boarding schools. His mother, Princess Alice of Battenberg, was suffering with mental illness, while his philandering father had abandoned the family. With parents like this, there were grave worries Philip would not remain faithful to Elizabeth.

There were also concerns about Philip's connection to the Nazis in the wake of World War II. All four of his older sisters had married Nazis, and when one of them, Cecilie, died in a plane crash in 1937, a young Philip was pictured at her funeral surrounded by Nazis.

Of course, it was also impossible to forget the domineering presence of Philip's uncle and mentor, Lord Mountbatten. Ambitious and determined, it was no secret that Mountbatten was actively campaigning in favour of the relationship - to the point where Philip apparently admitted that his uncle was placing a lot of pressure on him to ask for Elizabeth's hand in marriage.

It is said that Elizabeth's mother, Queen Elizabeth, referred to her future son-in-law as "the Hun" and that even Winston Churchill was suspicious of the prince. Though Elizabeth was excited about her future with Philip, her family secretly hoped that within a year she would have changed her mind.

Elizabeth may have been a naturally shy woman, but her family wholly underestimated her determination to marry Philip. Adamant that she would only marry him, King George and Queen Elizabeth were eventually forced to accept their daughter's relationship.

In the lead-up to the announcement of their engagement, Prince Philip renounced his Greek and Danish titles and became a naturalised British citizen, subsequently adopting the last name 'Mountbatten', a nod to his mother's British family. Philip also converted to Anglicanism in preparation for his marriage to the future Supreme Governor of the Church of England.

On the 9 July 1947, less than three months after Elizabeth's 21st birthday, the royal engagement was announced to the world. While the couple basked in happiness, it seemed that it was not only Elizabeth's family that had reservations about the match. A newspaper poll that was held soon after the announcement indicated that 40 per cent of the public were against the marriage – unsurprising, as Philip was considered too 'German' following the conclusion of the war.

Yet when it became clear that the couple were marrying for love rather than duty, those who initially opposed the marriage soon warmed to it. After all, a glamorous royal wedding was a welcome distraction for many in Great Britain and a great way to boost morale in the country.

With the wedding date set for 20 November and with just four months to plan the event, preparations quickly got under way. It wasn't until mid-August that the design for Elizabeth's wedding dress, by Sir Norman Hartnell, was approved, giving the renowned designer less than three months to create his masterpiece.

Wedding fever was running high throughout the nation (and worldwide), but with post-war austerity still in place, Elizabeth had to save up her clothing ration coupons in order to pay for the material for her dress – in total it took 3,000 coupons. To help her, hundreds of brides-to-be sent their own coupons to the princess so that she could use them. Although this was a very endearing gesture, the coupons all had to be returned to their owners as it would have been illegal for Elizabeth to use them because they belonged to others.

The government did provide Elizabeth with 200 extra coupons to pay for her wedding dress while Philip, never one for extravagance and spending, planned to wear his naval uniform for the big day. The couple would marry at London's Westminster Abbey, where Elizabeth's parents, King George and Queen Elizabeth, had married just over 24 years earlier, making the princess the tenth member of the royal family to wed in this spectacular setting.

It was decided that Elizabeth would have eight bridesmaids: her sister, HRH Princess Margaret, her cousin HRH Princess Alexandra of Kent, Lady Caroline Montagu-Douglas-Scott, Lady Mary Cambridge, The Hon. Pamela Mountbatten, The Hon. Margaret Elphinstone, Lady Elizabeth Lambart and Diana Bowes-Lyon.

As for Philip's best man, he chose David Mountbatten, the Marquess of Milford Haven, while Prince William of Gloucester and Prince Michael of Kent would serve as page boys. In total, 2,000 guests were to be invited to the wedding ceremony, many of whom were heads of state, such as Princess Juliana and Prince Bernhard of the Netherlands and the king of Iraq.

Notably absent would be Philip's sisters, as well as Elizabeth's uncle, the Duke of Windsor, who had

Elizabeth walking up the aisle at Westminster Abbey with her father

"WEDDING FEVER WAS RUNNING HIGH THROUGHOUT THE NATION"

caused a constitutional crisis just a decade earlier by abdicating the throne.

King George VI and his wife held a grand ball at Buckingham Palace just two days before the wedding to celebrate their daughter's upcoming marriage. The usually reserved King George even led a conga line through all of the state rooms in the palace. On the morning of the wedding, Prince Philip was made Duke of Edinburgh, Earl of Merioneth and Baron Greenwich. The day before,

Elizabeth and Philip are pictured here after announcing their engagement

King George had bestowed the title of 'His Royal Highness' on Philip, which meant that for a few hours the prince had the unusual title of His Royal Highness Sir Philip Mountbatten.

Philip had spent the night before his wedding at Kensington Palace, and with hordes of photographers outside in the bitter cold waiting for him to emerge, Prince Philip arranged tea and coffee for them. Meanwhile, Elizabeth was getting ready at Buckingham Palace, even applying her own makeup for the wedding.

Just like any wedding day, not everything went as smoothly as the princess would have liked. Her delicate bridal bouquet, delivered that morning and made of white orchids and a sprig of myrtle, had gone missing. The myrtle had come from Osborne House, where Queen Victoria had planted a cutting that had been given to her by Prince Albert's grandmother. As panic set in, it turned out that a footman had placed the bride's bouquet in a cool room to keep it fresh and prevent it from wilting.

The bouquet was not the only unfortunate mishap of the morning. Elizabeth's mother had lent her the Queen Mary Fringe Tiara to be her 'something borrowed' on her special day. Disaster struck as it was being placed on her head when the diamond tiara suddenly snapped. Standing by in case of an emergency was the court jeweller, who was rushed to his workroom by a police escort. Elizabeth waited anxiously and her mother quickly reassured her that the tiara would be fixed in time

An enduring love

DRESSING FOR THE DATE
Elizabeth's wedding dress was a sumptuous but modest creation perfect for the post-war years

Pearls fit for a princess
Elizabeth's double-strand pearls, gifted by her father, were actually two separate necklaces. The shorter one is known as the Queen Anne necklace and was said to have belonged to Queen Anne, while the second was known as Queen Caroline and was said to have belonged to the wife of King George II.

Patriotic patronage
The wedding dress was made with sumptuous duchesse satin, which had been sourced from the firm of Wintherthur, near Dunfermline in Scotland.

Elegant design
The dress had a simple cut with a fitted bodice and a heart-shaped neckline, with a low v-pointed waist and a floor-length panelled skirt.

Art inspiration
Hartnell stated that he had been inspired by Botticelli's famous painting *Primavera*, which symbolises the coming of spring – hence the applique motifs of flowers on the bridal train.

Bridal train
Elizabeth had a 15-foot full court train that attached on the shoulders and was made of silk tulle, embroidered with pearl, crystal and transparent applique tulle.

Dainty decoration
The dress was decorated with crystals and around 10,000 seed pearls, which had been imported from the United States. Meanwhile, the satin for the applique was produced at Lullingstone Castle in Kent.

Delicate shoes
Elizabeth wore ivory duchesse satin high-heeled sandals that were trimmed with silver and seed pearl buckles, made by Edward Rayne.

The beaming bride after her fairytale wedding

A ROYAL HONEYMOON
How Elizabeth and Philip spent their first few days as newlyweds

Elizabeth and Philip pictured in Malta following their marriage

As the bride emerged from Buckingham Palace to embark on her honeymoon, she wore a dress and velvet coat with a bonnet trimmed with ostrich feathers, designed by Norman Hartnell, in an appropriate shade of love-in-the-mist blue. The king and queen, along with Princess Alice, came out to wave the couple off.

Elizabeth and Philip were driven to Waterloo station in an open landau carriage so that the waiting crowds could see them – to ward off the cold, there were hot-water bottles on the floor of the carriage, along with Elizabeth's beloved corgi, Susan. As the carriage departed the newlyweds were showered with rose petals rather than traditional confetti.

Elizabeth and Philip travelled to Broadlands in Hampshire, the home of Philip's uncle Earl Mountbatten, where they spent the first half of their honeymoon in an 18th-century lodge – in 2007, the couple re-created their iconic honeymoon photo at Broadlands. Afterwards, they moved on to Birkhall Lodge, which was part of the Balmoral estate in Scotland, to see out the rest of their honeymoon.

While they were away, Elizabeth and Philip released a statement expressing the gratitude they felt for all the well wishes that they had received from the public. The princess also kept in touch with her family and lovingly informed her mother that Philip was "an angel".

"ELIZABETH'S DRESS WAS EXHIBITED AT ST JAMES'S PALACE BEFORE EMBARKING ON A TOUR"

– and it was. To top off the issues for the bride-to-be, the necklace that she was supposed to wear, a double strand of pearls gifted to her by her parents, had been put on display at St James's Palace. To get them in time, Elizabeth's private secretary raced to the palace, borrowing the car of King Haakon VII of Norway to make it in time.

Despite the bumps along the way, the princess and the prince were finally ready for their wedding, which was due to start at 11.30am. The royal parties arrived at the abbey in large carriage processions, past the thousands of onlookers who had lined the streets to get a glimpse of the royal bride. Queen Elizabeth and Princess Margaret were the first to arrive, followed by Dowager Queen Mary. Prince Philip left Kensington Palace accompanied by his best man and entered the abbey through a door near Poet's Corner. Meanwhile, Elizabeth made her way inside the decadent Irish State Coach, with her father by her side, escorted by the Household Cavalry. As the coach approached Westminster Abbey, the bells of St Margaret's Church rang out to announce the blushing bride's arrival. Outside, the princess was joined by her large bridal party. As the radiant bride made her way inside Westminster Abbey she must have been acutely aware that the entire ceremony was being recorded and broadcast by BBC Radio to 200 million people. Waiting at the High Altar was the Archbishop of Canterbury, Geoffrey Fisher, who officiated the wedding.

At the High Altar there were large vases filled with white lilies, roses, pink carnations, camellia foliage, variegated ivy and chrysanthemums. Clement Attlee, the prime minister at the time, and other politicians were sat in the choir stalls, with King George VI and Queen Elizabeth sat in the south side of the Sanctuary.

The organist and master of the choristers at the abbey, William Neil McKie, was the director for the music. The ceremony began with a fanfare specifically composed for the wedding by Arnold Bax, while McKie also composed a motet for the wedding, "We wait for thy loving kindness, O God." Sir Edward Cuthbert Bairstow sang a rendition of Psalm 67, and in total there were 91 singers with the combined choirs of Westminster Abbey, the Chapel Royal and St George's Chapel in Windsor.

The couple then exchanged their vows. Elizabeth's wedding ring was made from a nugget

An enduring love

Crowds lined the streets just to get a glimpse of the bride

The magnificent wedding cake

of Welsh gold, which came from the Clogau St David's mine, near Dolgellau. The gold had been given as a gift to Queen Elizabeth to make her wedding ring and, eventually, the wedding rings of Princess Margaret, Princess Anne and Princess Diana were all made with it.

After the couple finished their vows they moved into St Edward's Chapel behind the altar in order to sign their marriage register, accompanied by immediate members of their family. Once the register had been signed the couple walked out of the Abbey to Felix Mendelssohn's classic *Wedding March*.

Following the wedding ceremony the newlyweds returned to Buckingham Palace. The wedding breakfast was held in the Ball Supper Room at lunchtime, with a menu of "Filet de Sole Mountbatten, Perdreau en Casserole, and Bombe Glacée Princess Elizabeth". Princess Elizabeth, taking into account the post-war rationing of food, only had 150 guests attending the breakfast.

While the guests tucked into their food they enjoyed music provided by the string band of the Grenadier Guards. The delicate wedding favours were made from individual posies of myrtle and white heather from the royal estate of Balmoral in Scotland.

The stunning wedding cake was made by McVitie and Price. It was nine feet tall, separated into four tiers, and was made from ingredients that had been sent from all over the world. Even the sugar that was used had been provided by the Girl Guides in Australia, and as a result the cake was nicknamed 'The 10,000 Mile Cake'.

It was decorated with the arms of the bride and groom's families, monograms of the bride and groom, sugar-iced figures of their favourite activities and also decorations of regimental and naval badges. Elizabeth and Philip cut the cake with the sword that had been gifted to the groom by his new father-in-law.

Although this was the official wedding cake, the couple had received 11 wedding cakes in total. In fact, they received over 2,500 gifts and 10,000 telegrams of congratulations from well-wishers - Mahatma Gandhi had even sent a piece of cotton lace that he spun himself, embroidered with the words 'Jai Hind', or 'Victory for India', in English.

To greet those who had gathered on the Mall, Elizabeth and Philip made their way onto the balcony and waved to the adoring crowds. The next day, Elizabeth's wedding bouquet was sent back to Westminster Abbey to be laid on the Tomb of the Unknown Warrior, a royal tradition that had been started by her own mother when she had married in the wake of World War I.

The wedding fever that had consumed Britain did not end once the special day was over. Elizabeth's dress was exhibited at St James's Palace before embarking on a tour across the country, giving the public an opportunity to view it up close. The Palace also exhibited all of the gifts that the couple had received for the public to enjoy, while cinemas held screenings of the wedding ceremony across the country.

A couple of years into their marriage Philip relinquished his beloved and promising naval career in order to fully support his wife in her role as she assumed more responsibility in the wake of her father's declining health, proving to all that he would be a reliable and understanding consort to Elizabeth, who would become queen in 1952.

In 2007, Elizabeth became the first British monarch to celebrate a diamond wedding anniversary, and in 2017 the royal couple reached their platinum anniversary. Married for over 70 years, Elizabeth and Philip proved that love can overcome a host of challenges and last for a lifetime, and, given her warm tributes since his death on 9 April 2021 at the age of 99, beyond.

THE PRINCE OF HOPE

The birth of Prince Charles brought huge joy to his family, but his early years would see several separations from his mother and father

Words June Woolerton

If the marriage of the heir to the throne, Princess Elizabeth, to Prince Philip in 1947 had been billed as a celebration for Britain after years of wartime austerity, then the arrival of the couple's first child just under 12 months later was an added moment of sparkle for a country still dealing with the aftermath of war. However, the birth of this prince was also a pivotal moment for his family. A decade after the Abdication Crisis had called the very future of the monarchy into question, the House of Windsor was given a renewed strength by his birth, which secured the succession into the 21st century.

The royal wedding of 1947 had been a turning point for the royal family, and in the months that followed Elizabeth and Philip became the most celebrated members of the House of Windsor. An official trip to Paris in 1948 provided more glamour, but it also led to rumours that the princess was pregnant. She appeared pale and tired at an event and her husband whisked her out of one room so that she could rest. In June Buckingham Palace announced that the heir to the throne wouldn't be carrying out any more engagements from the end of that month - the rather discreet way that royal pregnancies were confirmed in the post-war years.

Elizabeth and Philip prepared for the arrival of their baby at Buckingham Palace, where they had been living for most of 1948. The young couple intended to move into Clarence House, but it was still undergoing major repairs while their planned country home, Sunninghill Park, had seen its main house lost to a fire. So the expectant parents passed the final months of Elizabeth's pregnancy with King George VI and Queen Elizabeth, who gladly helped oversee the plans for the birth of their first grandchild.

They also had to negotiate the title by which the new arrival would be known. Although Elizabeth was heir to the throne, her baby would take its title from its father, as only male-line grandchildren of a sovereign were automatically given royal status. Just days before the baby was born, King George VI ensured that his first grandchild would be royal from the moment of birth by issuing new Letters Patent, which confirmed the baby would hold the rank of HRH and the title of prince or princess.

A delivery room was set up in the Belgian Suite of Buckingham Palace. Named in honour of Queen Victoria's influential uncle, King Leopold of the Belgians, its three rooms were decorated with art by Canaletto and Gainsborough and among the pictures hanging on its walls were portraits of King George III and Queen Charlotte. The princess would end up spending several days there. Her labour began in the afternoon of Saturday 13 November 1948 but proved long and difficult.

Prince Philip, like many expectant fathers of the time, was kept outside the delivery suite, and as the labour progressed into a second day he took his anxiety out on the squash court. It was there that he heard news of the birth, which cemented the House of Windsor's hold on the throne.

The longed-for baby was born on 14 November 1948 after a 30-hour labour that ended with a Caesarean section, which had been carried out under general anaesthetic. However, the difficult delivery had been made easier by the decision to stop the practice that required the home secretary to be present to ensure the baby wasn't switched for another. Elizabeth gave birth safely and privately to her son at 9.14pm.

The baby was eventually delivered in the Buhl Room of Buckingham Palace, weighing 7lb 6oz and in perfect health. Prince Philip immediately opened champagne to start the toasts and was on hand with flowers for his wife when she eventually came round from her sedation.

The large crowd that had gathered outside for news of the royal birth had to wait a little longer to start their celebrations. The official announcement was pinned to the gates of Buckingham Palace just before midnight, and not long afterwards the arrival of the royal baby was broadcast on radio news bulletins.

In the hours after the baby prince's birth thousands of telegrams poured into Buckingham Palace offering congratulations from around the world. Bonfires were lit around the country to celebrate the arrival of a future monarch, following a tradition that had been kept for centuries. Outside the palace the crowds sang and partied into the small hours until they were asked to quieten their celebrations to allow mother and baby to rest.

The new second in line to the throne was soon ensconced in a nursery next to his mother's bedroom and spent his early weeks in quiet seclusion while the outside world continued to fete him with traditional gun salutes and peals of bells. Elizabeth was overjoyed with her son, writing to her aunt, May Elphinstone,

James Chuter Ede, home secretary from 1945-1951, was told just weeks before that his presence wouldn't be required for the birth of the heir to the throne's baby

THE PRIVATE BIRTH OF A PRINCE

For centuries politicians witnessed the heir's birth, but Elizabeth would give birth without them

As final preparations were made for the arrival of the longed-for heir, the home secretary, James Chuter Ede, was expected to attend the delivery to ensure that the baby wasn't substituted at the moment of birth. However, the idea seemed increasingly unnecessary and intrusive. When it was pointed out that a 1931 law meant that up to seven ministers from different parts of the empire might have to attend, King George VI decided to bring the tradition to an end.

It meant that Prince Charles became the first royal baby born without the presence of a politician for hundreds of years. Official witnesses to a royal birth had been compulsory since the end of the 17th century after the Protestant enemies of the Catholic King James II claimed that the healthy baby boy born to his queen in 1688 was actually a changeling.

Since then, queens and princesses had given birth with politicians in attendance. Queen Victoria decided in 1894 that just the home secretary would attend. By the early 20th century he was usually in a discreet position outside the door to allow the royal mother a degree of privacy, but he was still required to attend all deliveries.

The ending of this royal tradition in 1948 meant that the last baby to be born in the presence of a politician was Princess Alexandra of Kent. The House of Windsor's future monarch had begun modernising from the moment of Prince Charles's birth.

Elizabeth and Philip photographed with Charles and Anne

that the baby was "too sweet for words", adding that she could hardly believe she had a son of her own. Her mother Queen Elizabeth described her grandson as a "darling" baby. The little prince's other grandmother, Princess Alice, was living in Greece at the time of his birth and heard about his arrival in a telegram from her son. Her sister, Queen Louise of Sweden, also wrote to her, affectionately describing the infant prince as having "a little bit of fair fluff for hair". However, the outside world was kept waiting for a glimpse of the heir, with the first official portraits taken by royal favourite Cecil Beaton on 14 December, exactly a month after his birth. But even then there was no name to go with the face – that was to be kept secret until his christening.

On 15 December 1948, the archbishop of Canterbury, Geoffrey Fisher, baptised the second in line to the throne as Charles Arthur Philip George.

> "THE CROWDS SANG AND PARTIED INTO THE SMALL HOURS"

The baby had been carried into the service in the Music Room at Buckingham Palace wearing the Honiton lace christening gown first used by Queen Victoria and Prince Albert for their children. Fisher used water from the River Jordan for the baptism, which took place, as was traditional, at the gilded silver Lily Font. The prince, born to be king, was supported by eight godparents at his christening, among them two reigning monarchs. His godfathers included his proud grandpa King George VI, King Haakon VII of Norway, Prince George of Greece, and his great-uncle David Bowes-Lyon, the younger brother of Queen Elizabeth.

His godmothers were led by his great-grandmother Queen Mary, while his aunt, Princess Margaret, also stood sponsor. Philip's grandmother, Victoria, Dowager Marchioness of Milford Haven, was another godmother, with his cousin Patricia Brabourne completing the line-up.

The prince of hope

His Royal Highness Prince Charles of Edinburgh, as he was officially known, spent his first Christmas with his family at Sandringham. However, the New Year would bring big changes for the little prince. In July 1949, Clarence House was finally ready for its new residents after an extensive refurbishment programme led by the Duke of Edinburgh, which had drawn some criticism when it went over budget. So Charles left his grandparents' home at Buckingham Palace to move just round the corner with his parents. However, his parting from George VI and Elizabeth wouldn't last long.

The king's health had been giving cause for concern for some time. Two days before the birth of the boy who now stood to one day inherit his throne, George VI had been diagnosed with arteriosclerosis, which was so severe his doctors were concerned he might lose a leg. He had determined to keep his condition secret from Princess Elizabeth while she had her baby but shared the news soon afterwards.

After she had recovered from her difficult delivery, his heir found herself taking on more of her father's duties. Meanwhile, Prince Philip, who had longed to return to active service, had been made second-in-command of Chequers, part of the Mediterranean fleet. He left for Malta, with his wife following him not long afterwards. The baby Prince Charles was left with his grandparents.

Much of his day-to-day care was carried out by his nanny, Helen Lightbody, who was brought in to look after the little prince when he was a month old. Then aged 30, she had previously worked for the Duke and Duchess of Gloucester, supervising their two sons, Prince William and Prince Richard. Born in Scotland, she was known for her stern approach, which would later earn her the nickname 'No Nonsense Lightbody'. Her disciplined nursery became the centre of the young prince's world, and she was often seen pushing him through London's parks in his pram.

Charles was also cared for by Mabel Anderson, who joined the royal household as an under nanny in 1949. She was far more relaxed and fun than her stentorian boss, and the two women became important figures in the young prince's life. However, it was Queen Elizabeth who really took Charles under her wing. She clearly loved playing and spending time with her grandson and took charge of ensuring each birthday and Christmas he spent away from his parents was filled with many special moments to remember.

Years later, Prince Charles would talk about how his mother didn't spend as much time with him as he had wished and their first separation - as she headed to Malta - was longer than initially anticipated as Princess Elizabeth decided to extend her stay and enjoy Christmas on the island.

When she returned at the start of 1950 she spent several days in London catching up on her work before heading to Sandringham, where the toddler prince had spent Christmas in the company of his doting grandparents.

Charles's early years were filled with family fun. Here, aged around two, he plays hide-and-seek with his mother

A young Prince Charles poses with his grandmother, Queen Elizabeth. The two shared a very close bond

Although it was usual for upper-class families to spend time apart from their children, some US media reports criticised Elizabeth for her extended stays away after she headed back to Malta that spring for another break with her husband. When she returned she was in the early stages of her second pregnancy, and back home there were more calls on her time. As the health of George VI continued to cause concern, there were more responsibilities for his heir to take on, but she was also able to pass happy days with her baby son, who was soon to become a big brother.

However, Prince Philip was still in Malta and only returned to England in July 1950 to await the birth of the new baby. Princess Anne arrived on 15 August that year in a far more straightforward delivery that took place at Clarence House. Now in command of the frigate Magpie, Philip travelled back and forth between England and Malta in the following months, leaving for another extended stay after the christening of his daughter. Charles, who now shared his nursery with a sister, waved goodbye again to his mother in November as she headed out to join Philip. Although still young, the prince was spending less and less time with his parents and relying more and more on the attentions of his grandmother Queen Elizabeth, with whom he would always enjoy a close relationship.

The time he did spend with Philip would grow tense as the Duke of Edinburgh saw how sensitive Charles could be and tried to train it out of him by encouraging him to brush off problems in the same practical way that he himself had always found so effective. It would cause tension during Charles's childhood and real friction between the two men in later years. Philip was as likely to tell his young son to pick himself up and dust himself off as he was to offer cuddles and kisses after a tumble.

However, he was also a fun father, initiating hours of fun and games while he was at home. He was also quite clearly the head of their household, taking the lead in family matters even though his wife's role as queen-in-waiting was rapidly taking on more significance.

The birth of a king-in-waiting was announced with the traditional, simple bulletin pinned to the gates of Buckingham Palace

Princess Elizabeth and Prince Philip pose with Prince Charles and Princess Anne at Buckingham Palace in October 1950

In October 1951, Elizabeth's position as heir to the throne took the couple to Canada and the United States for an official tour that would keep them away from home for over a month and cause them to miss their son's third birthday. On their return to England, Charles was waiting for them at Euston station with his grandmother but had to take second place to the formalities, receiving a kiss from his mother and a pat on the head from his father after they had greeted Queen Elizabeth.

It was in another moment of separation that Prince Charles's childhood changed forever. His mother was in Kenya when, on 6 February 1952, her father died in his sleep and she became queen. Her son was now heir to the throne, with a new title of Duke of Cornwall and a new role that beckoned for him after a childhood that had started in the bliss of a cosy family life but had also entailed plenty of painful separations.

Soon after the birth of Prince Charles, his grandmother Queen Elizabeth wrote that "something as happy and simple and hopeful for the future as a little son is indeed a joy". As the House of Windsor contemplated a new era with yet more change to come, Charles remained the great joy of his family's life, but, as the heir they had always desired from Princess Elizabeth, he was also their great hope for the future of the royal lineage and Britain as a whole. With such enormous expectations came a great burden of responsibility that would soon come to weigh heavily on the young prince's shoulders.

The last summer of King George VI saw young Charles spend sunny days with his beloved grandparents

THE PRINCE IN TURMOIL

For young Prince Charles, school offered little emotional relief from his oppressed and lonely childhood

Words **Philippa Grafton**

In Gordonstoun, a young, troubled Prince Philip found the closest thing to home he had ever known. During a period defined by war, anguish and a divided family, Philip sought refuge at the strict, disciplinarian boarding school, which provided him with stability, structure and unity. It's little wonder, then, that when it came to his own children's education mere decades later, Philip turned back to the school that had saved him from the tragic reality of his own childhood. But where Philip thrived within the strict regime, Prince Charles cracked and crumbled under the pressure.

The firstborn son of Princess Elizabeth and her husband, Prince Charles was born on 14 November 1948, just six days shy of his parents' first wedding anniversary. While the pregnancy had passed without serious incident, Charles's birth was not an easy one. Princess Elizabeth was in labour for 30 hours before she was sedated and doctors opted to deliver the baby via caesarean section. Agitated by the long labour, Philip had been restlessly pacing around Buckingham Palace waiting impatiently for news until his private secretary, Michael Parker, insisted on playing a game of squash to take their minds off the birth. When word reached Philip that the baby had finally been delivered he sprinted to Elizabeth's bedside, bundled the newborn into his arms and declared that he looked like a "plum pudding". For the first few weeks of his life, Prince Charles was never far from his mother; the baby slept in the dressing room that joined the princess's bedroom, and she happily breast-fed her newborn, until she suffered a bout of measles in January 1949 and she was separated from her baby, handing him into the care of nannies and nurses.

This premature separation marked the first of many partings and disappointments for the young Prince Charles. With his father a celebrated naval officer and his mother the heir to the British throne, Charles's parents struggled to give their new child the attention that he so craved. Princess Elizabeth was determined to see her son daily; at 9am, the young boy would be brought to see his mother, and in the evenings - assuming her busy schedule allowed it - she would head to the nursery to spend time with her son before bedtime. Despite this, motherhood had put additional strain on an already stretched princess - not only was she expected to perform royal duties befitting a future queen, but she was a devoted daughter to her increasingly frail father and a loving wife to her husband, whose career was on the cusp of greatness. An undisputed war hero, Philip had shown great promise in his naval career, and it was expected that one day he would secure the coveted role of First Sea Lord. He was devoted to his job and was hellbent on achieving as much as possible before he would eventually be forced to give it all up upon the ascension of his wife.

The young couple were doggedly determined to live as normal a life as possible before the inevitable happened, and Philip's career called him out to Malta, where the pair resided for several months out of the year from 1949. In this peaceful Mediterranean haven Philip and Elizabeth managed to live a remarkably normal life, with the princess taking up a position with the Soldiers, Sailors, Airmen and Families Association charity. For the young, in-love couple, these carefree days were bliss; for their young son, who remained in the care of nannies, nurses and his grandmother back in the UK, these were the foundation blocks for a relationship defined by difference and distance.

What the young prince lacked in parental affection from Princess Elizabeth and Philip, he made up for in his close bond with his grandmother. A sensitive child who craved attention, Charles found the love he desired from the queen, who proved to be the young boy's closest companion throughout his childhood years. Although the queen had experienced a similarly distant relationship with her own children, usually only seeing them for mealtimes and before bed, Queen Elizabeth embraced her

Prince Charles was the first royal in British history to attend university, where he studied anthropology, archaeology and history at Cambridge

The Queen came to watch Prince Charles's first-ever sports day at Hill House in July 1957

role as doting grandmother, indulging her grandson to the point of spoiling him. She cultivated the young boy's passion for the arts, showing him the Royal Collection's finest paintings and allowing him to explore Windsor Castle. But in her lavish affection, Queen Elizabeth pandered to the young prince, which in turn encouraged Charles's bad habits, such as whingeing and self-pity. When he saw these traits in his son, Philip was so appalled that he sought to discipline them out of him.

Princess Anne, who had been born in the summer of 1950, was the polar opposite of her brother - in many ways, Anne was the son that Philip had hoped Charles could be. Anne was independent and wilful, humorous and sporty. This rough-and-tumble tomboy quickly won her father's praise, something that Charles had craved.

In February 1952, the inevitable finally happened. King George VI passed away, leaving the throne to his eldest daughter. It was a moment that the whole family dreaded - Elizabeth and Philip were forced to sacrifice the happy lives they had built for themselves in Malta. From their English residence of Clarence House they moved into Buckingham Palace, and Philip, the former head of the family, way usurped by his wife, the newly named Queen Elizabeth II.

With this change came additional responsibilities for the couple. Only a matter of months after Elizabeth's coronation in June 1953, the pair set off on a six-month Commonwealth tour. When they returned in the spring of 1954 they found their two children welcoming but aloof. According to the Queen years later, they "were terribly polite. I don't think they really knew who we were." In the months since their parents had gone away, the two children had continued to be brought up by nannies, the only difference to their daily lives the missing bedtime visits from their parents.

For the two young royals, their nannies had all but replaced their parents. Helen Lightbody loomed large in Prince Charles's childhood, running the nursery and taking care of the prince. It's rumoured that a young, inexperienced Elizabeth was fearful of the domineering older woman, who was as strict with Charles's mother as she was with the young boy. However, after allegedly incurring the wrath of the Queen in 1956, Lightbody was forced to resign. She was swiftly replaced by the younger Mabel Anderson,

The prince in turmoil

Prince Charles was flown to Gordonstoun by his father

"THE ROYALS QUESTIONED THE YOUNG PRINCE'S FUTURE"

who eventually took care of all of the Queen and Philip's children. In 1953 the family hired Catherine Peebles as Charles's governess, tasked with taking charge of the future monarch's early education. Catherine wasn't new to tutoring royalty; her previous job had been with the Duke of Kent's children. The governess's approach to teaching her young charge was soft but encouraging - she understood the young child's disposition and offered him praise and encouragement for doing well rather than reprimanding him for mistakes.

Sadly, Charles's happy days with Catherine were limited. It was soon decided that what Prince Charles really needed was the company of other children, something he could only truly benefit from by attending school. With that in mind, the prince became a pupil at Hill House in Kensington at the end of 1956. He became the first heir apparent to be sent to public school.

At Hill House, Prince Charles found himself treated like any of the school's other students. He was noted for enjoying drawing and painting, and he proved himself more than capable at reading and writing. He particularly excelled at music. What he struggled with, however, was maths. Although the young boy was only at the school for a few months, he attended the school's sports day at the end of the academic year in 1957, captured on film introducing his mother to his fellow pupils, who duly shook hands and bowed.

From Hill House, Prince Charles began to take his tentative first steps in the same direction as his father. In September 1957, Charles took up a place at Cheam School, a strict boarding school in Hampshire that Philip had attended. He struggled to make friends, instead finding himself a target for the school's bullies, and he was stricken by homesickness. His troubles at the school continued when, the following year, he was summoned to the headmaster's office with several other students. Here, the boys were allowed to watch the Commonwealth Games in Cardiff on the TV. In a speech made at the Games, the Queen revealed that she had decided to bequeath her son the title of Prince of Wales - a revelation that took the prince by surprise and left him rather embarrassed, especially when the boys in the room turned to him to congratulate him.

Life at Cheam continued much the same - with the very occasional caning for bad behaviour - but behind the scenes the royal family were questioning Charles's future. With his time at Cheam drawing to a close, a decision needed to be made on where to send him next. Two schools caught the attention of the royals: Eton College in Windsor, or Gordonstoun in the north of Scotland. Both schools had vocal supporters, with Prince Philip backing his own alma mater, while the Queen Mother voiced her support for Eton, but the final decision lay with Queen Elizabeth. Ever her grandson's most supportive companion, the Queen Mother insisted that Charles should attend Eton, writing to the Queen in May 1961, "I have been thinking such a lot about Charles. I suppose that he will be taking his entrance exam for Eton soon. I do hope he passes because it might be the ideal school for one of his character and temperament. However good Gordonstoun is, it is miles and miles away and he might as well be at school abroad." Assured that her opinion could sway her daughter, she continued, "All of your friends' sons are at Eton and it is so important to be able to grow up with people you will be with later in life. And so nice and so important when boys are growing up that you and Philip can see him during school holidays and keep in touch with what is happening. He would be terribly cut off and lonely in the far north."

What the Queen Mother hadn't bargained for, however, was her son-in-law's determined grit and insistence on having some semblance of authority within his own family. Philip rebutted the Queen Mother's argument by claiming that Charles would be harassed by the media were he to go to Eton.

With his parents often away, the young prince grew close to his grandmother, the Queen Mother

Photographed here in 1958 while he attended Cheam School, Charles was mocked mercilessly for his protruding ears

Like Gordonstoun, Timbertop challenged the prince, but he felt more accepted there than at his previous schools

While studying at Gordonstoun Charles indulged in his passion for drama, here playing Macbeth in a 1965 rendition of the Shakespeare play

What the boy needed was solitude and independence – at Gordonstoun, Charles would find himself and thrive, just as Philip had done three decades before him. In the end, Elizabeth sided with her husband and Prince Charles's fate was sealed.

In May 1962, Prince Philip piloted a plane and flew his son to an RAF base near the school, then drove him to the gates of Gordonstoun. With the knowledge that the heir to the throne was about to attend this remote school, two or three boys who knew Charles had been enrolled at the school in an attempt to make the transition easier, but several rule changes at the school in the lead-up to the prince's arrival thwarted any chance Charles had of settling in comfortably. Misdemeanours that previously went unpunished or slipped under the radar, such as drinking and smoking, suddenly carried heavy penalties – being caught smoking could result in a caning, while being caught drinking could lead to expulsion. Another rule that was forced upon students was that any antagonistic behaviour towards Prince Charles may result in expulsion.

Resentment mounted against the new pupil, and by the time he moved into his new accommodation in Windmill Lodge, he was the most despised student on campus. Any student seen being friendly towards the prince was mercilessly mocked and accused of sucking up to him. Despite the rule against mistreating him, Charles found himself once again a target for bullies, who allegedly attacked him in his sleep and verbally abused him. In February 1963, Charles wrote to his grandmother to exclaim, "I hate coming back here and leaving home; I hardly get any sleep at the House because I snore and get hit on the head the whole time. It is absolute hell." Letter after letter followed, complaining of the cruelty the young prince suffered at the hands of his schoolmates. "He was crushingly lonely for most of his time there," recalled a fellow student years later. "The wonder is that he survived with his sanity intact."

For several years, Charles endured the trials and tribulations of Gordonstoun, finding occasional joy in the performing arts. In 1965, Prince Charles was elated to play the lead in *Macbeth*, which his parents came to see. To his bitter disappointment,

The prince in turmoil

During his time at university Charles indulged his passion for music by playing the cello for Trinity College's orchestra

Prince Charles was stripped of his sailing privileges but also his closest companion after underage drinking in Stornoway

THE 'CHERRY BRANDY' INCIDENT
How one wrong foot sent Charles spiralling back to square one

In his second year at Gordonstoun, at the age of 14, Charles had the pleasure of joining the school's sailing team, with whom he experienced some semblance of freedom. However, the luxury was to be short-lived when one minor misdeed on an excursion catapulted him to nationwide infamy.

Having sailed to Stornoway Harbour, the young crew were given permission to explore the shore. However, the sight of Britain's next king in town set tongues wagging, and a crowd quickly began to gather. While his protection officer, Donald Green, had gone to buy the boys cinema tickets, Charles sought refuge in a hotel, descending deeper into the building to hide away from the attention. The room he found himself in, however, proved to be a bar. When the bartender asked what he wanted to drink, Charles blurted out "Cherry brandy" – the "first drink that came into my head… because I'd drunk it before when it was cold out shooting," he later lamented. Unknown to the prince, however, a journalist happened to be seated nearby. This typical teenage rebellion made headline news the next day.

As punishment, Charles was stripped of his sailing privileges, and his protection officer, who had supported the young prince throughout his terrible ordeal at Gordonstoun, was fired. "I have never been able to forgive them for doing that because he defended me in the most marvellous way and he was the most wonderful, loyal, splendid man," Prince Charles retorted many decades later.

"IN AUSTRALIA, CHARLES WAS JUST AN ORDINARY STUDENT"

Charles could hear his father's guffaws during one particularly emotive scene. Allegedly when the prince asked what his father was laughing at, Philip cuttingly replied, "It sounds like The Goons."

In February 1966, Philip made the decision to send Charles to study in Australia for a few months. Charles was flown out to Geelong Grammar's Timbertop campus, a remote school that challenged him in new and more exciting ways than Gordonstoun. The school prided itself on challenging its students physically, encouraging them to take part in outdoor activities like chopping trees, camping and going on cross-country treks. With the teenager Philip had sent his equerry, David Checketts. Remarkably, considering how badly Charles had settled in at his previous schools, he found life more than bearable in Australia. Here, fellow students and teachers cared little for Charles's title; he was just another ordinary student and was treated as such. During the week he worked hard at school and made friends, while his weekends were spent with his father's equerry and family, enjoying some semblance of a normal life.

"I went out with a boy and came back with a man," David famously stated of the prince's Australian sojourn. As well as finding himself, Charles's trip to Australia provided him with his first real taste of what it meant to be a royal. He performed his royal duties admirably, attending dozens of events and perfecting the art of talking to the crowds, as well as officials and politicians. When the time came to leave Timbertop, students gave a rousing cheer for the "real Pommy bastard" in typical friendly humour.

Despite his traumatic experiences at Gordonstoun, when Charles returned for his final year he found himself elected head boy, a surprise honour that nobody had really expected. With just months until his graduation

Stuart McGregor, a pupil at Timbertop, was assigned to welcome Prince Charles to the school. The pair became friends and kept in touch, reconnecting face to face at the old school in 2005

The prince in turmoil

The Free Wales Army was a nationalist group determined to secure Welsh independence

"CHARLES WAS PRAISED FOR HIS DILIGENCE AND TALENTS"

from the school he'd so despised, the question once again arose about Charles's future. After some debate, it was decided that Charles would attend university – specifically Trinity College at Cambridge, where he chose to study anthropology, archaeology and history. In October 1967, Charles arrived at his new residence, a second-floor flat on campus. Next door stayed David Checketts, who had since been assigned as Charles's own equerry.

Charles might not have been as academically gifted as his fellow students, but he was praised for his diligence and talents by his tutors, and after his first year he was on track for a 2:1. What Charles truly loved, however, was acting, and he delved into the university's creative side with gusto. As well as joining the famous Footlights Dramatic Society, he took part in college theatrics and joined Trinity College's orchestra, where he played the cello. Despite embracing university life, Charles still longed to be outdoors. "Any excuse to escape Cambridge and plod across ploughed fields instead of stagnating in lecture rooms is enormously welcome," he wrote to a friend after attending a shoot in January 1969.

In anticipation of his investiture as Prince of Wales in 1969, Prince Charles was to be pulled out of Cambridge and sent to the University College of Wales in Aberystwyth to become acquainted with Welsh language and culture. However, unrest had spread throughout Wales in the run-up to the event, with a nationalist group called the Free Wales Army – modelled on the IRA – planting bombs across the country in the previous years. Succumbing to the threats of a terrorist organisation was not an option, however, and Prince Charles was duly sent to live at Pantycelyn Hall. Despite the chaos, Charles threw himself into understanding his new principality. He empathised with the Welsh, writing to a friend that "they are depressed by what might happen to [Wales] if they don't try and preserve the language and the culture, which is unique and special to Wales, and if something is unique and special, I see it as worth preserving." On 1 July 1969, Prince Charles's investiture was televised across the country. With the threat of a terrorist attack still very much a possibility, the ceremony went ahead, but with Prince Charles wearing bulletproof gear beneath his regalia.

In June 1970, Charles became the first British royal to earn a university degree when he graduated from Cambridge with a 2:2 Bachelor of Arts degree. With his formal education at an end, the prince was free to pursue a more traditional royal education: military service. In an interview with *The Observer* in the 1970s, Charles reflected on his years of school turmoil: "I didn't enjoy school as much as I might have, but that was only because I'm happier at home than anywhere else." Alongside his military education, Charles faced another, very particular challenge: the hunt for a suitable wife with whom he could create his very own home.

THE INVESTITURE OF A PRINCE

The formal ceremony recognising the newest Prince of Wales was an occasion for celebration, but it also became a paramilitary target

Words **Scott Reeves**

Charles knelt before the Queen, who clasped his hands in hers. It was a moving moment between mother and son, but it was far from a private one. An audience of 4,000 looked on in reverential silence while footage from television cameras was beamed to millions more around Britain and the world. This ceremony, when Charles publicly assumed his title as Prince of Wales, would be the most meaningful of his life until his own coronation as monarch.

The investiture of the Prince of Wales at Caernarfon Castle was a relatively new procedure, deliberately designed to appeal to the masses. Yet Charles's celebration took place amid a backdrop of Welsh nationalism, with protests and paramilitary action threatening to ruin the royal pageantry.

By the time the investiture ceremony took place, Charles had already been Prince of Wales for more than a decade, having been granted the title (along with the Earldom of Chester) at the age of nine through letters patent issued by the Queen, who announced the move in a speech closing the 1958 British and Commonwealth Games in Cardiff.

The investiture ceremony was not necessary for Charles to be able to hold the title; many of the 20 previous Princes of Wales had been invested in Parliament, but the ceremony had fallen out of favour in recent centuries. However, the Queen's speech in Cardiff also declared her intention that Charles would be presented to the Welsh people at Caernarfon "when he is grown up".

Elizabeth was referencing a revived version of the investiture ceremony, the brainchild of David Lloyd George, who, as Chancellor of the Exchequer, wanted to celebrate the granting of the title to Prince Edward with a pageant at Caernarfon Castle in 1911. That Lloyd George was also Constable of Caernarfon Castle and the local MP no doubt contributed to his desire for his home patch to host a huge royal spectacle.

Charles grew from a boy into a young man in the 11 years between being made Prince of Wales and the investiture ceremony on 1 July 1969, completing his schooling and beginning classes at Trinity College, Cambridge. As part of the preparation for the upcoming investiture, he spent nine weeks at the Aberystwyth campus of University College of Wales, studying the history and language of his principality. The purpose of the decade-long delay was to ensure that Charles fully understood the significance of his position as Prince of Wales, and he commented before the investiture, "For me, it's a way of officially dedicating one's life or part of one's life to Wales." He would later declare that he wished to "associate myself with as much of the life of the principality as possible. As a result of my two-month stay in this country, I have come to see far more in the title I hold, than hitherto."

On the day of the ceremony the royal train arrived at a specially built platform at a disused railway station near Caernarfon Castle. Charles disembarked and travelled to the castle in an open-top carriage separately from the rest of his family and awaited their arrival in the Chamberlain Tower. The Queen and the Duke of Edinburgh followed on, entering the castle and stepping onto the stage in the grounds accompanied by the Earl of Snowdon (Charles's uncle and Constable of Caernarfon Castle), the Marquess of Cholmondeley (Lord Great Chamberlain), the Duke of Norfolk (Earl Marshal) and the Gentleman Usher carrying the Great Sword of State. The Duke of Norfolk instructed Sir Anthony Wagner, the Garter King of Arms, to fetch the prince from the tower.

Accompanying Charles as he processed to the stage were 11 dignitaries, including Owen Lloyd George, grandson of the driving force behind the revived investiture ceremony. Charles knelt before the stage and its three thrones: one for the Queen, one for the Duke of Edinburgh and one left empty. The Queen handed copies of the letters patent to the Home Secretary (and future prime minister) James Callaghan and Welsh Secretary George Thomas. Both read them out to the 4,000 assembled guests - Callaghan in English, Thomas in Welsh.

As the Welsh proclamation was being read the Queen presented Charles with the Honours of the Principality of Wales: a girdle and sword, a gold ring, a gold rod, a mantle and, most importantly of all, a coronet. The headwear referenced that of the last Welsh prince, Llywelyn ap Gruffudd, whose coronet was seized after his death by Edward I during the conquest of Wales. The design was recorded by Charles II in 1677 as a "coronet of crosses and fleurs-de-lis with one arch and a ball and cross". New versions were made in 1728 for Prince Frederick and in 1902 for Prince George, although the most recent coronet was taken by the

Charles described the oath of loyalty as the most meaningful moment of the day

PRINCE EDWARD TO PRINCE CHARLES

Charles was the latest prince to be granted an 800-year-old title

King Edward I created the title of Prince of Wales in its current form when he granted it to his son in 1301

The title that Prince Charles was granted in 1958 and invested in 1969 had a long history. The last Prince of Wales who was actually Welsh was Llywelyn ap Gruffudd, killed by the forces of King Edward I in 1282. Almost 20 years later, Edward revived the title for his son, a symbolic gesture that indicated Wales was now under his control. Legend says that the king promised the Welsh chieftains a prince who was born in Wales. To keep his promise, he presented them with his own son who was born at Caernarfon Castle. He then rubbed salt in the wound by using the coronet of Llywelyn in the investiture ceremony.

The first English Prince of Wales did not give his own son the title upon becoming Edward II, but Edward III did, and it soon became a title traditionally given by monarchs to their eldest son and heir apparent. More than 800 years later, Charles became the 21st Prince of Wales - 14 of whom have subsequently succeeded to the throne - and on 8 September 2017 he surpassed Prince Edward (later King Edward VII) as the longest-serving prince.

---

former Edward VIII when he abdicated and went into exile. Although the ex-king had no right to take the coronet with him, it was decided impolitic to threaten him with judicial action and the treasure was only returned upon his death in 1972. Since Prince Frederick's 241-year-old coronet was judged to be too fragile, a new one was manufactured by the Worshipful Company of Goldsmiths and presented as a gift to the Queen for Charles to wear.

Now wearing the regalia of his new title, the Queen wrapped her hands around her son's while he declared, "I, Charles, Prince of Wales, do become your liege man of life and limb and of earthly worship, and faith and truth I bear unto you, to live and die against all manner of folks." Charles later described it as "by far the most moving and meaningful moment" of the day. Monarch and prince exchanged a kiss of fealty and Charles sat down on the empty throne to listen to a loyal address from the people of Wales delivered by Sir Ben Bowen Thomas (President of University College of Wales, Aberystwyth). The prince then stood to deliver two speeches, one in Welsh and one in English. After a brief religious service, the 30-minute investiture was concluded.

With the ceremony complete, Charles walked with his parents to Queen Eleanor's Gate to wave to the 90,000-strong crowd on the streets Caernarfon. A 16-plane RAF flypast soared over the heads of the throng before the royal party returned to the train station.

Monarch and newly invested prince may have soaked up the cheers of the crowd, but not everybody was supportive of the ceremony. Nationalism was a growing movement in Wales. Plaid Cymru had been founded in 1925 to campaign for Welsh independence through the political system and won its first seat in Parliament in the 1966 Carmarthen by-election. Plaid members created the Cymdeithas yr Iaith Gymraeg (Welsh Language Society) in 1962 to promote the use of Welsh throughout the principality and enthusiastic graffiti artists painted over English-language road signs.

Nationalist fervour was particularly stoked by the decision to flood the Tryweryn Valley to create

Charles's investiture as Prince of Wales would be one of the most important royal ceremonies of his life

"INTELLIGENCE SUGGESTED THAT A SNIPER MIGHT TRY TO TAKE A POT-SHOT AT THE PRINCE"

The investiture of a prince

Caernarfon Castle was selected as the location due to its historical links to the first Prince of Wales and Lloyd George's efforts to revive the investiture in 1911

a reservoir and pipeline carrying water to Cheshire and Liverpool. The inhabitants of Capel Celyn were forced from their homes in 1965 and the submerged village became a symbol for those who thought Welsh interests were being ignored in favour of England.

Harold Wilson's Labour government hoped to dampen nationalist zeal with a year-long campaign called Croeso (Welcome) '69 based around the investiture to promote investment in new industries. Coal mining was in decline and the youthful heir to the throne was seen as the ideal figurehead for a new Welsh chapter. However, many objected to the creation of a Prince of Wales who had little personal connection to the principality. A satirical song complained that Charles was rarely seen in Wales: "Charlie, Charlie, Charlie's playing polo today / Charlie, Charlie, Charlie's playing polo with his daddy / Join in the song / Subjects big and small / We finally have a prince in the land of song."

A few boos were heard as the royals travelled to Caernarfon Castle and a couple of eggs were thrown towards the Queen's carriage. That was embarrassing, but of far more concern were militants who were prepared to use violence to achieve their aims. In 1952, Y Gweriniaethwyr (The Republicans) hit the headlines when they attempted to blow up a pipeline that ran from the Claerwen Dam in Powys to Birmingham. The bomb was especially worrisome since it was designed to go off as Elizabeth II opened the dam, one of her first official acts since succeeding to the throne.

The Free Wales Army sought media attention by fostering links with the IRA and Basque separatists, while Mudiad Amddiffyn Cymru (Movement for the Defence of Wales) planted a series of bombs throughout the 1960s that targeted dams, pipelines, the electricity network and civic offices. Hopes that the investiture of Prince Charles would not be a target were soon dashed. A bomb exploded at the Temple of Peace and Health in Cardiff on the day before an investiture planning meeting was to take place there in 1967.

The paramilitary threat led to a huge security operation around the investiture. 250 extra police officers patrolled the streets, while 4,000 soldiers were billeted nearby. Manhole covers were sealed and balconies were cleared when intelligence suggested that a sniper might try to take a pot-shot at the prince. Radio stations were surrounded with barbed wire while the Royal Engineers were on standby to repair any damage. Despite the precautions, some nationalists were not deterred. The evening before the investiture, Alwyn Jones and George Taylor, two members of Mudiad Amddiffyn Cymru, were killed when a bomb they had been placing outside government offices in Abergele exploded prematurely.

Just as the investiture finished, Charles heard a distant explosion when a bomb planted in a local constable's garden exploded. When the Welsh Secretary told him it was a royal salute, the

The coronet was manufactured specially for the investiture after the previous version was pilfered by the abdicated Edward VIII

prince replied that it was a peculiar salute. "There are peculiar people up there," the Welsh Secretary said. Another explosive was planted in an iron forge near Caernarfon Castle; a final bomb was placed on Llandudno Pier to stop the Royal Yacht Britannia from docking since the prince was scheduled to board the ship for a four-day tour of the principality after the investiture. Both bombs failed to explode.

Yet despite the actions of the paramilitaries, they remained a vocal minority. Around three-quarters of Welsh people supported the investiture taking place (although some were concerned about the expense) and many held street parties to mark the occasion. The ceremony aimed to further boost the standing of the royal family and was designed to make full use of the relatively new medium of television. After the success of Elizabeth's coronation in 1953, in which 20.4 million people watched at least half an hour of the service - this in a country with only 2.7 million television sets - the royal family realised that television could be harnessed to broaden their appeal.

The Queen's Christmas message was televised for the first time in 1957, and she allowed cameras to record her for a year between June 1968 and May 1969, with the resulting 110-minute documentary, *The Royal Family*, being shown on both BBC and ITV in the weeks before the investiture. Viewers were able to see the private lives of the Queen's household for the first time, including the royal family enjoying leisure time. When the Duke of Edinburgh took control of the family barbecue, Charles made the salad dressing.

The investiture of a prince

ROYAL REGALIA
The investiture ceremony saw Charles presented with the magnificent honours associated with his title

Coronet: A symbol of his rank as a prince, Charles wore on his head not a crown (which is reserved for the monarch) but a coronet.
Sword and girdle: Symbolising Charles's right to dispense justice, the grand sword first used in the 1911 investiture of Prince Edward has a hilt in the shape of a coronet supported by two dragons.
Rod: Long used as a representation of the right to rule, the rod decorated with dragons illustrated Charles's governance over the principality of Wales.
Ring: A token of unbreakable union similar to a wedding ring, the gold ring given to the prince symbolised that Charles had committed himself to Wales
Mantle: Charles's robe was a garment traditionally worn by royalty. Like the other items of regalia (apart from the coronet) it was first used in the 1911 investiture.

The Earl of Snowdon, who oversaw planning for the investiture, adapted the 1911 programme of events to make its ceremony more suitable for television. A plain grey slate stage meant that it was easier for people to see what was happening on a grainy screen. The vagaries of the British weather meant that it was necessary to have a cover - even in July there was always the possibility of rain - but Snowdon ensured that a clear plastic canopy was used so the views would not be blocked. The Queen and Charles had rehearsed over and over in the garden at Buckingham Palace to ensure they stood in the correct places for the cameras, a mock-up Caernarfon Castle courtyard marked out with tape on the floor.

Coverage on BBC One began at 10.30am in the morning and continued until 4.30pm in the afternoon. Those who had new PAL-compatible television sets could tune into BBC Two, which carried the live broadcast in colour. In total, 19 million watched the coronation in Britain, although viewing figures ballooned to 500 million when including those who watched around the world.

When Charles had time to look back on his investiture and the preparation that went into it, he recorded in his diary, "Last week has been an incredible one in my life and it now seems very odd not to have to wave to hundreds of people... I now seem to have a great deal to live up to and I hope I can be of assistance to Wales in constructive ways." The Prince of Wales had turned from a boy into a man by publicly assuming his royal title. Now he needed to find a role to go with it.

Charles posed for official portraits in his regalia to mark the investiture

Charles's first naval posting came aboard HMS Norfolk, although his guests soon proved he was not a typical junior officer

CADET TO COMMANDER

The six years Charles spent in the armed forces were among the busiest and toughest in his life

Words **Scott Reeves**

On 8 March 1971, an apprehensive Charles landed on the runway at RAF Cranwell in Lincolnshire to begin serving his mother in a military uniform. The heir to the throne was a little late in beginning the customary period in the armed forces carried out by male members of the royal family – he broke with convention to continue his education to graduate level – and it has been suggested that he was initially an unwilling recruit who had to be persuaded by his father to join up. However, once the decision was made, Charles threw himself into a busy six-year term of active service.

It was immediately obvious that Charles was not a typical cadet. He had already received flying instruction from instructors during his second year at Cambridge University, earning a private pilot's licence, and he was at the controls of the plane that took him to Cranwell, giving him a head-start on his colleagues that allowed the year-long course to be condensed to just five months. Having a prince on base meant extra security precautions were put in place too, although he was still expected to adhere to the pecking order and address senior officers as 'Sir'.

Charles thrived in the military environment, perhaps unsurprisingly since it mirrored the hierarchy of the royal family and boarding schools in which he was raised. The mathematical nature of some of the desk-bound courses proved tricky, but it was all worthwhile for the feeling of "power, smooth, unworried power" that Charles had when he was at the controls of a Jet Provost. The Prince also learned to fly the Chipmunk basic pilot trainer and the Beagle Basset multi-engine trainer.

Charles earned his wings on 20 August 1971 and spent a few weeks with his family at Balmoral before returning to the military classroom. This time, he was training under the aegis of the Royal Navy, following in the footsteps of his father, grandfather and two great-grandfathers.

Charles undertook six weeks of instruction at the Royal Naval College in Dartmouth, this time compressed from the usual three months, but the shortened course meant that Charles struggled to pick up the intricacies of navigation. Nevertheless, he ticked off seamanship, leadership, engineering and administration and was soon on his way to the island of Gibraltar to join HMS Norfolk on his first active posting.

The newest sub-lieutenant was housed in the same small cabin as others of his rank, although he was inevitably treated a little differently. Although he did his best to join in the occasionally rowdy escapades of his fellow junior officers, Charles was just as likely to be cooped up in his cabin keeping an unusually detailed naval journal that he meticulously recorded throughout his five years at sea.

No other sailors had personal protection officers when they went ashore, nor were they put through a demanding programme of one training course after another. Charles was shown the skills required of a commanding officer, including communication, gunnery and navigation (which still proved difficult to grasp), as well as how to escape from a submarine and riot control.

After seven months at sea, punctuated with a short period of leave to attend the Duke of Windsor's funeral at Windsor Castle, Charles returned to more naval courses on dry land, including intense one-to-one tuition at the Maritime Warfare School at HMS Dryad in Portsmouth. Charles's second posting saw him join HMS Minerva in December 1972, a smaller ship that required him to take on greater responsibilities. The tour of duty took him across the Atlantic, and Charles combined his on-ship officer's duties with the need to act as his nation's ambassador when Minerva stopped at various ports of call in the Caribbean, North America and South America. He was present during the celebrations as the Bahamas gained independence from the British Empire; Grenada would follow the next year.

After finally gaining his watch-keeping and ocean-navigation certificates, Charles was promoted to lieutenant. Yet more courses followed before Charles flew to Singapore to join up with HMS Jupiter and her tour to the Far East. As communications officer, Charles no longer had to worry about dreaded navigation, and the ship's itinerary gave him a chance to take in the 1974 Commonwealth Games in New Zealand.

On her return voyage, the ship had a week-long stop in San Diego that enabled Charles to hobnob with Governor Ronald Reagan (who impressed him), Frank Sinatra (who did not) and experience the spark of romance with Laura Jo Watkins, a daughter of US Admiral James Watkins. However, any hopes that a relationship would blossom were swiftly quashed due to the fact that, as a Catholic, Watkins was considered an unsuitable wife for the heir to the British throne.

When Turkey invaded Cyprus in July 1974, the potential arose for Charles to fire shots in anger – he craved "some sort of action" and the chance to prove himself in battle. However, Jupiter was quickly diverted away from the Mediterranean. It was decided that the heir to the throne should be kept away from an active theatre of war and his frigate was despatched to Scotland for NATO training exercises instead. "I never had a chance to test myself," Charles would later lament, but the opposition of both the royal household and admiralty was implacable.

Charles took to the sky again in the autumn of 1974, completing the course that made him a qualified helicopter pilot in December. Charles had been promised the chance to fly with 845 Naval Air Squadron operating from HMS Hermes and began the three-month deployment in March 1975.

Charles finally had a chance to relax away from the endless slog of training courses when he was given an eight-month break from active duty after his deployment on Hermes. His military career was increasingly incompatible with his other royal interests and Charles spent much of his leave preparing for the launch of the Prince's Trust.

Aware that his next military posting would be his last, Charles was given command of the coastal minehunter HMS Bronington in February 1976. The top brass selected an experienced bunch of officers to serve under him – the last thing they wanted was anything going wrong during the culmination of Charles's military career – and Bronington embarked on a largely incident-free tour in the waters around the UK. Charles's active service ended with a report commending his "excellent level of professional competence" amid "enormous outside pressure".

Charles's time in the armed service was a little artificial. His training was condensed and rushed; he was given special leave to fulfil royal obligations; and it was impossible for the heir of the throne to fit neatly into the strict hierarchy without some special treatment. However, the experience and credibility that Charles gained during his time as an officer would prove invaluable in his later royal role, giving him an opportunity to mingle with seamen from all walks of life and outside his usual exclusive circles.

After six years in uniform, Charles found it difficult to completely step back from the armed services. Despite no longer being on active service, Charles added to his long military CV when he completed the Parachute Regiment's basic training course. Charles, appointed colonel-in-chief of the Parachute Regiment in 1978, decided it would be inappropriate to lead them without undergoing the training himself despite being 30 years old, considerably older than his fellow trainees.

The fact Charles was in his fourth decade did not phase his parachute-jumping instructors but it was beginning to play on the minds of his royal advisers, who pushed Charles to end his career in the armed forces. They wanted him to steer away from military courses and look to earn a different type of certificate: one that recorded his marriage.

Charles flew planes in the Queen's Flight for more than 20 years before voluntarily giving up his licence

BACK TO EARTH WITH A BUMP
Charles's wings were clipped following a heavy landing

Charles's first flights at Cambridge University and Cranwell led to an enduring fascination with the air and, after his military career came to a close, he continued to log flying hours with the Hawker Siddeley Andover, Westland Wessex and BAe 146 of the Queen's Flight, often getting on with work during the flight and taking the controls for landing. That came to an abrupt end, however, on a windy summer morning in the Inner Hebrides.

Charles was aboard the Queen's BAe 146 when he took over at the invitation of the aircraft's captain and came in to land on the Isle of Islay. Charles landed too fast, bursting three tyres and causing the plane to slide across the runway, coming to rest with its nose in mud. None of the six passengers or five crew were injured but damage to the nose cone, landing gear and weather radar cost around £1 million to fix.

Aware that it could have been far worse – the plane ended up at a right-angle on the runway, 18 metres from a drop into a stream – Charles voluntarily chose to give up flying. He would return to being a passenger rather than a pilot.

Charles spent six busy years serving in his mother's armed forces

Cadet to commander

By becoming a helicopter pilot Charles blazed a trail that would be followed by his brother Andrew and sons William and Harry

LOVE

42 **Sowing his wild oats**
Once the most coveted bachelor on the planet, the future king enjoyed the company of several potential suitors before meeting Diana

52 **Prince Charles & Diana Spencer**
The marriage of Charles and a pretty young nanny gave Britain a real-life fairytale to celebrate

58 **A prince is born**
The arrival of Prince William in the summer of 1982 provided Charles with an heir and was met with widespread joy by the country

64 **Hurrah for Harry**
Despite the birth of their second son, Charles and Diana's marriage was slowly eroding

68 **On the rocks**
Straining to keep up appearances, it soon became clear to the world that the Prince and Diana's marriage was floundering

72 **The end of a fairytale**
Amid a storm of salacious headlines, the couple's marriage finally came to an end in 1992

SOWING HIS WILD OATS

Prior to marrying Diana, Princess of Wales, Charles was one of the most eligible men in the world, with a whole host of girlfriends behind him

Words Catherine Curzon

There are few men more eligible than the heir to a throne and in the 1970s one of the most eligible of all was Charles, then the Prince of Wales. Once a shy, bullied child, by the time he was grown Charles was flourishing. He was a keen sportsman and dedicated member of the forces, and there was no shortage of single women keen to make the acquaintance of the king-to-be.

Charles was encouraged to "sow his wild oats" by his great-uncle, Lord Mountbatten, who encouraged his nephew to enjoy as many affairs as he could before he was a husband. As a father figure to the young prince, whose relationship with his father, the Duke of Edinburgh, was never particularly close, Mountbatten's encouragement and occasional intervention to do some matchmaking of his own was welcomed by Charles. Soon that once-timid young man was to be found with a seemingly endless parade of well-bred and exceptionally eligible young ladies on his arm.

One of those women would stick. Though both married others, Charles and Camilla eventually reunited and made their relationship official, but the road to respectability was rocky for Charles and marked by the weight of expectation and duty. On one side was the royal family itself, keen for the heir to the throne to make a marriage that would be respectable and appropriate. When Charles was Prince of Wales, that ideally meant someone of a similar social standing, so the net was cast wide for a young woman from an impeccably respectable and aristocratic - or perhaps even royal - family. On the other hand was Mountbatten, sending his great-nephew highly personal letters in which he encouraged him not to bow to pressure to marry too early but to cast his own net before marriage came along to keep him in line.

There were even some parents who tried to do some fruitless matchmaking of their own. Among them was Richard Nixon, who ensured that Charles was in the constant presence of his daughter, Tricia, when Charles made an official visit to the White House in 1970. In other cases, most notably Sheila Ferguson of the Three Degrees, Charles's crush became a flirtation that apparently went no further.

Though Charles did his best to enjoy as many relationships as he could, some casual and some more serious, the vast majority of his partners came from the rarefied world of the aristocracy. That's hardly surprising considering the social set in which he moved, but what might be more surprising is the sheer number of women involved. Whether Charles was having fun or genuinely searching for the woman he could spend the rest of his life with is open to interpretation. One thing is certain: Charles was determined to take his great-uncle's advice and sow his wild oats while he still had the chance.

THE FIRST GIRLFRIEND
LUCIA SANTA CRUZ
YEAR OF BIRTH: 1943
WHEN DID THEY DATE? 1968-1970

Charles was studying at Cambridge University when he met the woman who was to become his first real girlfriend. When the Master of Trinity College, Rab Butler, noticed that the young undergraduate seemed shy around women, he introduced him to his own research assistant, Lucia Santa Cruz. Five years Charles's senior, Lucia was the daughter of Chile's ambassador to Britain and she boasted a formidable intellect as well as a bubbly, engaging personality. Charles was smitten, and for two years the couple were a casual item.

Though Charles took her to meet his family at Balmoral, Lucia's Roman Catholic faith meant that there were never any hopes of marriage between the then Prince and the woman who introduced him to the delights of female company. Ironically, Lucia also introduced Charles to Camilla Shand, who lived in the same apartment block as the Chilean. Lucia shrewdly told the prince that Camilla was "just the girl" for him and history, of course, proved her right. The trio have remained friends ever since.

After her stint at Cambridge, Lucia Santa Cruz returned to Chile and married lawyer Juan Luis Ossa. Not only was she was invited to the wedding of Charles and Camilla, but when Prince William and Kate Middleton tied the knot, the prince's father's old friend was among the guests invited to the Westminster Abbey ceremony.

The intelligent and accomplished Lucia Santa Cruz was Charles's first serious girlfriend

Wildlife filmmaker Cindy Buxton was devoted to her career

THE AMBITIOUS EXPLORER
CINDY BUXTON
YEAR OF BIRTH: 1950
WHEN DID THEY DATE? 1967-1970

Lucinda 'Cindy' Buxton dated Charles on and off during his years as a Cambridge undergraduate, but her focus was firmly on her career rather than the heir to the throne. As the daughter of Lord Buxton of Alsa, Cindy Buxton could boast an impeccable pedigree, but though her relationship with Charles lasted for several years, it was never really serious enough to give the royal family cause to suspect it might become permanent. In fact, Cindy had already discovered her vocation and was set to follow her father, who had created the ITV series *Survival*, into the world of wildlife documentaries.

Cindy Buxton released her first wildlife documentary film in 1971 at the age of 21. Since then she has enjoyed a highly successful and distinguished career, travelling the world extensively and winning plaudits for her films. She lived for a long period in Africa, was caught up in the Falklands War while filming for a documentary, and later released a book regarding her hazardous journey through Antarctica. Her work in the field of wildlife and environmental documentaries has earned Cindy many plaudits and she even has a glacier named after her in recognition of her environmental work.

Now happily married, Charles and Camilla enjoyed an on-off relationship for years

CHARLES'S SOULMATE
CAMILLA SHAND
YEAR OF BIRTH: **1947**
WHEN DID THEY DATE? **1971-1973**

Not long after she split from her boyfriend and future husband, Andrew Parker Bowles, Camilla Shand was introduced to the then Prince of Wales by their mutual friend, Lucia Santa Cruz. She and Charles hit it off immediately and their close friendship eventually developed into a romance. Camilla and Charles had a huge amount in common, including a passion for polo that allowed them to spend time together at matches in Windsor Great Park, where they mingled with a privileged social set. Though their friends thought the couple were perfect for each other, Camilla wasn't quite what the royal family were looking for and Charles's passion for her didn't turn into a proposal.

It was a surprise to the couple's friends when their apparently ideal relationship came to an end in 1973, and unsurprisingly neither has ever explained what caused the split. Some believed Charles told Camilla not to wait for him when he was posted overseas, others that the royal family intervened and had him sent abroad in order to end the relationship and clear the way for a more aristocratic woman. Camilla eventually married Andrew Parker Bowles, though she and Charles later rekindled their relationship as an affair. Camilla's marriage to Parker Bowles ended in 1994 and she and Charles finally married in 2005.

MOUNTBATTEN THE MATCHMAKER
Charles never had the closest relationship with his late father. Instead, he turned to his great-uncle, Lord Mountbatten, for guidance

Lord Louis Mountbatten, 1st Earl Mountbatten of Burma, was renowned as the matchmaker who had brought Prince Phillip and Elizabeth II together. He fully intended to use those skills again when it came to Charles.

Charles called Mountbatten his "honorary grandfather", and for Charles, whose relationship with his father was often strained, his great-uncle was a father figure too. Mountbatten was convinced that Charles should sow his wild oats while he still had the chance and believed that if he did then he would be satisfied when the time came to marry. He also advised his great-nephew to marry a virgin - as royal protocol demanded - and warned him that a woman who had had other lovers would not thrive when placed on a pedestal as the Princess of Wales. Mountbatten hoped Charles would choose Mountbatten's granddaughter as his bride, but that wasn't to be.

Sowing his wild oats

THE FRIENDLY FLING
ROSIE CLIFTON
YEAR OF BIRTH: **1952**
WHEN DID THEY DATE? **1973**

Rosie Clifton was one of a number of casual flings that Charles enjoyed once his relationship with Camilla had ended in the early 1970s. Rosie was the daughter of a colonel, and while she was certainly never a serious contender for the position of Princess of Wales, she and Charles were well-matched as friends. She also loved all things horsy and they were part of the same equestrian set, so their brief relationship in the autumn of 1973 was a natural progression.

When Charles and Rosie ended their short-lived romance she moved on to a far more serious relationship and subsequently married the Honourable Mark Vestey, the younger brother of Baron Vestey. Vestey was a talented polo player but his career was sadly ended at the age of 41 when a hunting accident left him paralysed from the chest down. Rosie nursed her husband back to health and continued to be a familiar figure both in equestrian circles and at charity events alongside her husband, who became High Sheriff of Gloucester following his accident. Rosie Vestey was widowed in autumn 2016. She was joined at her husband's memorial service by senior members of the royal family including Camilla.

Though she and Charles were good friends, Rosie Clifton was never a contender for his heart

THE ADMIRAL'S DAUGHTER
LAURA JO WATKINS
YEAR OF BIRTH: **1953**
WHEN DID THEY DATE? **1974**

In the early spring of 1974 Charles embarked on one of his more unusual romances during a visit to San Diego, where he was to serve aboard HMS Jupiter as part of a goodwill mission to the US. It was during this trip that he met Laura Jo Watkins, the daughter of Admiral James Watkins. Admiral Watkins just happened to be very close to Lord Mountbatten, having met him in Malta in the 1950s.

Laura Jo was unlike the parade of short-lived aristocratic girls who caught Charles's, eye, and for a few months he was smitten. Though her Roman Catholic faith meant that Laura Jo would never have been able to marry him, for a brief time they were inseparable. When Charles returned home on leave, Mountbatten issued an invitation to Laura Jo to visit England as his guest. Of course, it was really so she could spend more time with Charles.

Charles invited Laura Jo to watch his maiden speech in the House of Lords and her presence became the hottest talking point in the media, supposedly much to the chagrin of senior royals. When she was nowhere to be seen at a polo match later that week, Charles laughed, "You don't think I'm such a bloody fool as to bring her here today, do you?"

Laura Jo's relationship with Charles faded after that, though she joined him for a polo weekend in Deauville and was present at his marriage to Diana. Laura Jo has since married and lives in New York as Laura Jo Kauffman.

Charles was smitten with American Laura Jo and even invited her to watch him speak in the House of Lords

THE ECCENTRIC AUSSIE
DALE 'KANGA' HARPER
YEAR OF BIRTH: 1948
WHEN DID THEY DATE? 1974-1997

Known as 'Kanga', Australian-born Dale Harper boasted no title, but she was raised in privilege. She was known for her colourful personality and love of life, and when she arrived in England she swiftly entered the upper echelons of society thanks to her friendship with Anthony Tryon, 3rd Baron Tryon, who eventually became her husband. It was Charles's friend, Baron Tryon, who introduced her to Charles, who famously said that Kanga was "the only woman who ever understood me", and their relationship supposedly continued even after she had become Baroness Tryon.

Lady Tryon launched a successful fashion business named Kanga in the early 1980s and even managed to convince Diana, Princess of Wales, to wear one of her creations to the famous Live Aid concert of the time. Lady Tryon suffered from recurring serious health problems as she grew older, which were exacerbated by her reliance on alcohol and prescription drugs. She was left paralysed by a fall from the window of a rehabilitation clinic, which some commentators claimed was an attempt at suicide.

Kanga was divorced from Baron Tryon in 1997 and was subsequently sectioned. After her release she took up residence in the Ritz Hotel. She died aged just 49 as a result of septicaemia.

Colourful and eccentric, Australian-born Lady Tryon was known to her friends as Kanga

For a short while in the 1970s, it seemed as though Davina Sheffield was the woman who would capture the eligible Prince

THE ONE THAT GOT AWAY
DAVINA SHEFFIELD
YEAR OF BIRTH: 1951
WHEN DID THEY DATE? 1975-1976

Though most people believe that Camilla was the one that got away - for a time at least - there was actually one other serious contender for Charles's heart. In 1976, Davina Sheffield, the daughter of an army major and granddaughter of Lord McGowan, came very close indeed. This society beauty was already in a relationship when she was introduced to Charles by his sister, Princess Anne, and he fell head over heels for her. Though their relationship began platonically, Charles provided a much-needed shoulder for Davina to cry on following her mother's murder, and soon their friendship turned to love.

Known not just as a society beauty but also for her philanthropic work in Vietnam, Davina split from her boyfriend and became a regular companion of Charles's, leading friends and journalists alike to speculate that a proposal was on the cards. Davina even lunched with Elizabeth II and spent a summer weekend with the royal family at Balmoral, which was considered proof of her royal companion's intentions. As the press clamoured for more information about the glamourous young lady, her ex-boyfriend happened to mention to a reporter that he and Davina had briefly lived together. In one fell swoop her suitability as a possible Princess of Wales and future queen came to an abrupt end. No candidate for the position of royal bride could be seen to have previously "lived in sin", let alone be anything other than a virgin.

Davina later married and, as Mrs Morley, went on to raise three sons.

Sowing his wild oats

Despite fevered press speculation, Lady Jane Wellesley had no intention of marrying Charles

THE ART MAGNATE
LADY ANGELA NEVILL
YEAR OF BIRTH: **1948**
WHEN DID THEY DATE? **1975**

Though Davina Sheffield's past history left her out of the running as a potential bride for the then Prince of Wales, Lady Angela Nevill's could not have been more perfect. She was the daughter of Lord Rupert Nevill, the private secretary to the Duke of Edinburgh, and was also a goddaughter of the Queen herself. Lady Angela's life had been entirely without scandal and she had built herself a reputation for intelligence and business acumen, building her own highly successful art consultancy up from nothing. Lady Angela specialised in purchasing paintings, gathering their provenance and selling them on at a vast profit to her wealthy clients all over the globe.

Though Charles and Lady Angela were undoubtedly well-matched when it came to intellect and background, the closeted life promised to the future Princess of Wales had no attraction for a successful professional such as she. Instead, she and Charles ended their relationship, continuing as just friends.

Angela married her business associate, Billy Keating, in 1994, and was his wife until his death four years later. She continues to be one of the more celebrated and successful art dealers in the world, regularly dealing in vast sums of money and securing priceless works of art for her clients.

Lady Angela Nevill was a member of the royal inner circle and one of Princess Margaret's bridesmaids (third from left)

THE MEDIA-SHY CAREER WOMAN
LADY JANE WELLESLEY
YEAR OF BIRTH: **1951**
WHEN DID THEY DATE: **1976-1977**

Few of Charles's girlfriends were considered so perfect a candidate to become the Princess of Wales as Lady Jane Wellesley, the daughter of the Duke of Wellington. Her pedigree was ideal, as was her background and upbringing, but she loathed the media spotlight that was shone on her relationship with the then heir to the throne.

When Lady Jane joined Charles at Sandringham to see in the New Year, a crowd of 10,000 gathered to await the apparently inevitable announcement of their engagement. The announcement never came, and when one intrepid journalist asked Lady Jane if there was to be an engagement between herself and Charles, her response was unequivocal. Rather than give a media-friendly reply, she snapped, "Do you honestly believe I want to be queen?"

The relationship between Lady Jane and Charles had both the approval of Elizabeth II and plenty of passion too. In fact, Charles was rumoured to spend the night at Lady Jane's London home while his bodyguard slept outside in the car. When the relationship subsequently ended, it was widely assumed that Jane's dislike of the limelight had been the driving factor, not to mention her outspoken personality and unwillingness to toe the line of a royal wife.

Lady Jane Wellesley became neither a queen nor a wife, despite a relationship of nearly a decade with Melvyn Bragg. Instead she focused on her own career as a biographer. When asked if she regretted not becoming the Princess of Wales she responded archly that she didn't need another title as she already had one of her own.

Lady Sarah Spencer's relationship with Charles ended after she gave a tell-all exclusive to reporters

THE SISTER-IN-LAW
LADY SARAH SPENCER
YEAR OF BIRTH: 1955
WHEN DID THEY DATE? 1977

Lady Sarah Spencer was the granddaughter of Earl Spencer and was viewed as an eminently suitable candidate for a girlfriend of the then Prince of Wales. In 1977, Spencer introduced her new boyfriend to her sister, Lady Diana, but though Lady Sarah later described herself as Cupid, it was several years before Charles and the sheltered Diana met each other again.

During her relationship with Charles, Lady Sarah spoke to two reporters in a restaurant and naively handed them an exclusive in which she discussed her anorexia, alcoholism and her numerous previous boyfriends. Perhaps most damaging of all, she admitted to keeping a scrapbook on her romance, an admission that led the journalists to conclude that Lady Sarah was in fact in love with fame.

When the article was published Charles was apoplectic and their short relationship fizzled out soon afterwards. Though some speculated that Lady Sarah was jealous of Diana following her marriage, she was actually one of her sister's closest confidantes and often accompanied her as a lady-in-waiting.

Lady Sarah married Neil McCorquodale in 1980 and together they have three children. Following the death of Diana, Princess of Wales, she was one of the foremost female influences in the lives of her two young nephews, William and Harry.

THE CONTROVERSIAL ACTRESS
SUSAN GEORGE
YEAR OF BIRTH: 1950
WHEN DID THEY DATE? 1978

In a world of aristocratic and titled women, actress Susan George rather stood out from the pack. Born not in a stately home but Surbiton, she began her career as an actress at the age of four and was educated at stage school, while she famously spent her holidays at a Welsh caravan park.

By the time Charles and Susan George began their relationship she was already a celebrated and sometimes controversial actress, especially for her role in Sam Peckinpah's *Straw Dogs*. She burst onto the British social scene in the wake of her flourishing career and Charles found her delightful company, though her background obviously meant that she was never in with a chance of marriage. Though their relationship was never confirmed, they have remained friends ever since. When asked later about her rumoured romance with the then heir to the throne, Susan refused to confirm it but simply said that Charles was a very special and valued friend.

Susan George married actor Simon MacCorkindale in 1984 and the couple were together until his death in 2010. Though her appearances on stage and screen are sporadic nowadays, she continues to enjoy a very successful career as a breeder of Arabian horses.

With childhood holidays spent on a caravan park, Susan George never stood a chance at making it to the altar

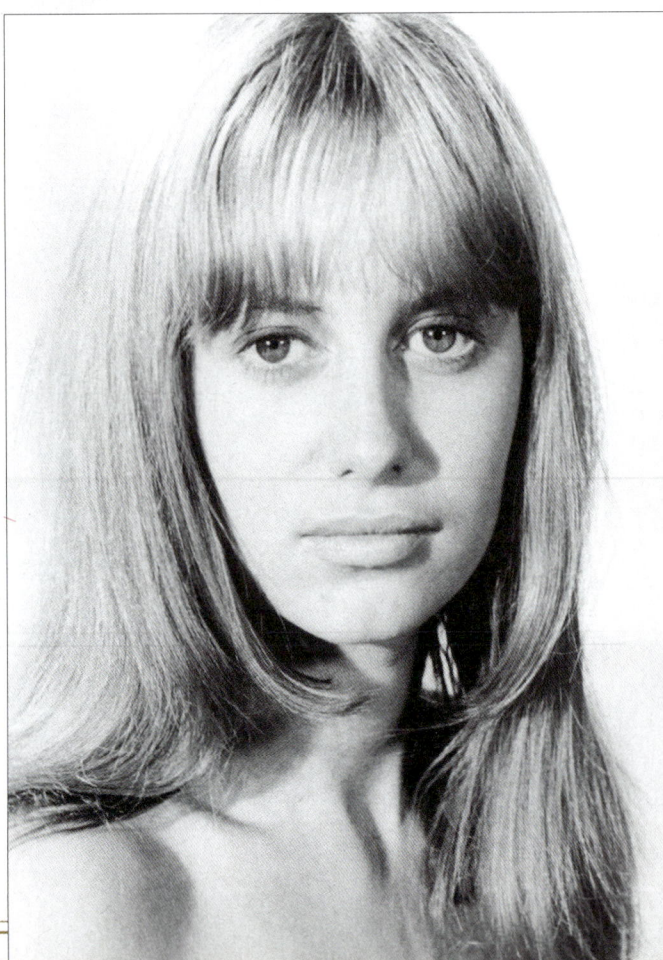

Sowing his wild oats

THE SOCIALITE HEIRESS
SABRINA GUINNESS
YEAR OF BIRTH: **1955**
WHEN DID THEY DATE? **1979**

By the time she met Charles in 1979, socialite Sabrina Guinness was famed not only for her privileged life but for how wild it had been too. This granddaughter of Sir Arthur Guinness had already enjoyed high-profile relationships with Mick Jagger, Rod Stewart and David Bowie, among others, and was the heiress to the Guinness fortune.

Though her infamous past meant that Sabrina was never likely to win the approval of the royal family, the besotted Charles still invited her to spend a weekend with them at Balmoral. She and Charles enjoyed secret dates together and she even learned to fish so she could accompany him on trips to the shoreline. The couple had been together for nine months when Charles ended their relationship, apparently due to his family's reservations about Sabrina's past. Rumour has it that both of Charles's parents were not always welcoming when she joined royal gatherings.

Following the end of the affair, Sabrina remained unmarried for over three decades and continued to enjoy relationships with a string of famous - and infamous - men. Once celebrated as an it-girl, she devoted her time to philanthropic work in later years and founded a charity devoted to training disadvantaged youths to work in the media. She finally tied the knot in 2004 when she became the wife of playwright Tom Stoppard.

MARRIAGE – ROYAL STYLE
When it comes to royal marriage, love just isn't enough

When divorcee Meghan Markle married Prince Harry, much was made of her normal background. Once, not so long ago, the idea of a member of the royal family marrying a commoner was virtually unheard of, and for an heir to the throne it was doubly so. Whoever was to marry the man who was Prince of Wales was expected to one day serve as his queen. It wasn't a job for the faint-hearted.

In addition to an excellent pedigree, the one thing that wasn't up for negotiation was the virginity of the bride-to-be. There could be no ex-lovers to sell their stories and Shy Di, as the press termed her, fit the criteria perfectly. There were even rumours that she'd had her virginity confirmed by a royal surgeon! Today, thankfully, such archaic rules no longer exist, and the virginity of a royal bride - never her husband, of course - is no longer a subject of media speculation.

> "NOT SO LONG AGO, THE IDEA OF A ROYAL MARRYING A COMMONER WAS VIRTUALLY UNHEARD OF"

THE MATCHMAKER'S FAVOURITE
LADY AMANDA KNATCHBULL
YEAR OF BIRTH: 1957
WHEN DID THEY DATE? 1980

In 1974, Lord Mountbatten suggested his 17-year-old granddaughter, Lady Amanda Knatchbull, as a perfect match for Charles. Her mother, Lady Brabourne, liked the idea but asked Charles to wait until her daughter was a little more mature and ready for marriage.

Mountbatten waited until 1979, when he arranged for Lady Amanda to join him and his great-nephew on Charles's forthcoming official tour of India. His efforts were frustrated by Lord Brabourne, who feared that sending the second cousins on the trip together would cause a media frenzy that could potentially end the relationship before it began.

In 1979, Lord Mountbatten was killed along with Amanda's youngest brother and a crew member when an IRA bomb detonated on a boat they were travelling out to sea in. Charles undertook his tour alone and returned in 1980 to propose to Lady Amanda. Some saw it as a desperate act, as Charles had always intended to be married by 30, yet he was still single when that birthday came. Lady Amanda turned down the proposal, having no wish to join the royal family.

A social worker by profession, she has become a leading figure in her field, specialising in child protection. She married Charles Ellingworth in 1987.

A grieving Amanda Knatchbull turned down Charles's proposal

THE KENNEDY FAVOURITE
HELGA WAGNER
YEAR OF BIRTH: 1942
WHEN DID THEY DATE? 1980

Helga Wagner was a celebrity jewellery designer who was a confidante of the Kennedys

Although Charles usually liked to stick to aristocratic British ladies when it came to his companions, he occasionally opted for someone who was a little less his typical type. Among those women was Austrian Helga Wagner (née Mayerhofer), who had set up home in Florida and founded a successful jewellery design studio that boasted clients including Jackie Onassis and Princess Caroline of Monaco. She brought with her a wealth of intrigue and was a Kennedy favourite. In fact, she was the first person Edward Kennedy phoned after his notorious car accident at Chappaquiddick. She was also a divorcee, having parted from her husband, Robert Wagner, six years before she and Charles met.

Charles and Helga met at a dinner in Palm Beach, where Charles asked the host to change the seating plan so that he could squire her to the table and have her undivided attention all night. The following day Helga was his guest at a polo match, but when he invited her to holiday with him in the Bahamas she pled a previous engagement.

Helga Wagner's glamour appealed to Charles, as did the fact that she represented a complete change from the supposedly appropriate girlfriends whom he socialised with at home. Helga married artist Helmut Coller and she continues to design and sell jewellery from her Palm Beach store today.

> "CHARLES USUALLY LIKED TO STICK TO ARISTOCRATIC BRITISH LADIES WHEN IT CAME TO HIS COMPANIONS"

Sowing his wild oats

Diana met Charles when she was just 16, but it would be several years before they started dating

THE WOMAN WHO SAID NO
ANNA WALLACE
YEAR OF BIRTH: **1955**
WHEN DID THEY DATE? **1980**

Known to her society friends as 'Whiplash Wallace' thanks to her hot temper and equestrian skills, Anna Wallace was the heiress daughter of a Scottish landowner. Charles adored the striking young woman and was so determined to make her his wife that he proposed to Anna twice. She rejected him on both occasions.

The relationship between Anna and Charles faltered after the press revealed the details of her former love life, but it was Anna who took the initiative and ended it once and for all. At a ball given in celebration of Elizabeth The Queen Mother's 80th birthday, Charles ignored Anna and danced with the married Camilla Parker Bowles all night instead, leading Anna to tell him that she had never been treated so badly in her life. When Charles left Anna standing on the edge of the dance floor as he partied with Camilla at a polo club dance later that month, she ended the relationship there and then.

Within weeks of their split, Charles began dating Diana and Anna married the late Johnny Hesketh, brother of Lord Hesketh. Following their amicable divorce she married financier Tom Oates in 1991 after a four-week courtship. That marriage ended in 2007.

Glamorous and fiery, Anna Wallace walked out on Charles when he ignored her in favour of Camilla

THE NURSERY TEACHER TURNED PRINCESS
LADY DIANA SPENCER
YEAR OF BIRTH: **1961**
WHEN DID THEY DATE? **1980-1981**

Though Charles had always declared that he intended to be married by the age of 30, he ended up missing his self-imposed deadline by a few years. Instead of a bride, he accumulated a long list of former girlfriends in his search for the perfect princess.

In fact, Charles had known the lady in question for years. Lady Diana Spencer and Charles had first met in the late 1970s when Diana was just 16 and Charles was dating her sister, Sarah. It wasn't until they met again at a polo event in 1980 that she became a serious contender for the position of Princess of Wales.

Diana's background was perfect. She was from an aristocratic family, had no ex-boyfriends or scandal lurking in her past and was everything that the royal family had been looking for in a match for Charles. They invited Diana along to family events, including a weekend aboard the royal yacht Britannia and a trip to Balmoral estate, where she met and charmed the prince's parents and grandmother.

With the blessing of his family, Charles began to court the nursery school teacher who was 13 years his junior and lacked his romantic experience. He proposed in February 1981, beginning one of the most tumultuous and well-documented relationships in the history of the royal family. Of all the women in Charles's past, only one ever went extensively on the record about their relationship. That woman just happened to be his first wife, the woman who despite her 'perfect' background rocked the royal family.

PRINCE CHARLES & DIANA SPENCER

The wedding of Prince Charles and Lady Diana Spencer was hailed as a real-life fairytale, but behind the scenes, things were already looking less than rosy

Words **Melanie Clegg**

When Charles, eldest son of Queen Elizabeth II, celebrated his 30th birthday in November 1978, speculation about who would be his future wife quickly intensified. Dubbed the 'Playboy Prince' by the press, Charles had had several girlfriends over the years, some deemed more suitable than others, but as far as anyone outside his close circle of friends and family knew he had not seriously considered marrying any of them - although he had unsuccessfully proposed at least once, to Lady Amanda Knatchbull, the granddaughter of his great uncle and mentor, Lord Mountbatten. In 1977 he was briefly involved in a relationship with Lady Sarah Spencer, the vivacious eldest daughter of Earl Spencer, but it quickly fell apart when Lady Sarah spoke to the press about him. However, before their relationship went awry Charles was invited to a shoot at Althorp, the country seat of the Spencer family, and it was there that he met Sarah's youngest sister, Lady Diana, who was just 16 years old and still at boarding school. Charles was intrigued by Diana's adolescent gaiety and high spirits and, after partnering her in a dance at the ball held at Althorp that evening, asked her to show him the Spencer family's famous picture gallery - only for Lady Sarah to unceremoniously intervene. Charles quickly forgot the youngest Spencer girl, but Diana was infatuated and could talk of nothing else but Charles for quite some time to come, even covering her bedroom walls with pictures of him.

Charles and Diana would not meet again until November 1978, when he invited her to his 30th birthday party. However, another 18 months would pass before they started to become romantically involved, when Diana was invited to attend a house party at Petworth in July 1980, allegedly at the instigation of Camilla Parker Bowles, a married woman with whom Charles had been having an on/off relationship for several years. According to Diana, Charles 'leapt' on her after she told him how sad she had felt when she watched him walking in the procession at Lord Mountbatten's funeral in 1979. It seemed to her, she told him, he needed someone to look after him, and Charles, who had come to the same conclusion, could not help but respond to her sympathy.

Shortly afterwards, Charles invited Diana to join him on the Royal Yacht Britannia for the annual Cowes sailing week in August - although this was far from being a romantic interlude, for she was part of a sizeable party and had her own cabin for the event. Indeed, Diana's virginal inexperience and previously very uneventful love life - which had gone no further than being chastely squired to society balls by old Etonians that she had known all her life - was considered to be very much in her favour by those close to Charles.

Things moved quickly after this. Diana was invited up to Balmoral a month later, which was taken as a strong sign that Charles was seriously interested in her. Meeting the Queen and the rest of the royal family on such an intimate level would be extremely daunting for most young women, especially one as shy and awkward as Diana was at that point, but she had known them all of her life thanks to her family's close relationship with them. In fact, Diana had been born in Park House on the Sandringham estate (her family lived there before her father inherited the Spencer earldom), while her formidable grandmother, Lady Fermoy, was one of the Queen Mother's closest friends.

Charles and Diana's wedding was a fairytale extravaganza, but their public smiles and happiness masked secret tensions and concerns about the marriage's future

Diana's world-famous engagement ring was chosen from a jewellers' catalogue rather than being custom-made

AN ICONIC ENGAGEMENT RING

Diana's beautiful sapphire and diamond engagement ring raised eyebrows in royal circles

Prince Charles did not come prepared with a ring when he proposed to Lady Diana Spencer in February 1981, but instead she was invited to choose her own ring from a selection at the royal jewellers, Garrard. Unusually for a royal engagement ring, it was not custom-made for her but was picked from their current stock, which raised a few eyebrows. Featuring 14 solitaire diamonds surrounding a 12-carat blue Ceylon sapphire set in 18-carat white gold, it cost £28,000, which is roughly equivalent to £98,000 now, although its current value is more like £300,000. Diana would always be very fond of sapphires and apparently chose this particular ring because of its enormous size, although she may also have been influenced by the fact that the design was allegedly inspired by the very similar diamond and sapphire brooch that Prince Albert presented to Queen Victoria as a wedding gift in 1841.

After Diana's death, the ring was inherited by Prince Harry, but he passed it on to his brother, William, so that he could give it to Catherine Middleton when they became engaged in 2010, believing that using his late mother's ring was a way of involving her in his engagement.

Although she would later claim to have disapproved of the match, it seems likely that Lady Fermoy was actually very much in favour of it and was responsible for Diana's next invitation to visit the royal family at Balmoral, this time staying with the Queen Mother at her private estate, Birkhall. Prince Charles was extremely close to his grandmother and, knowing that she was very keen that he should marry as soon as possible, was clearly hoping that she would approve of Diana. Luckily the visit went well, with Diana charming everyone with her good nature, prettiness and high spirits, and Charles took the next step of asking her to accompany him on a visit to Highgrove, the country house that he had recently purchased in Gloucestershire. Diana, who was used to the splendours of Althorp, found it a bit unimpressive and would have been even less thrilled if she had known that its primary attraction for Charles was its close proximity to Camilla Parker Bowles' country house.

Although Diana would later claim that she only met Charles 13 times before they became engaged, in reality they saw rather more of each other, with several meetings in London as well as trips to Balmoral, Highgrove and Sandringham, where she was a guest at a small royal gathering for Charles's 32nd birthday in November 1980. It was at around this time that news of their relationship broke in the press and Diana began to be hounded by photographers, who followed her wherever she went, while the newspapers were rife with speculation that an engagement was imminent. In the end, the much-expected proposal took place on 3 February 1981 at Windsor Castle, with Diana allegedly being so overwhelmed that she thought Charles was joking and burst out laughing before saying yes. News of the engagement was greeted with mingled happiness and relief by the royal family but was kept secret for a few more weeks while Diana spent some time alone with her mother in Australia. Later she would ruefully recall that this was the "last time I walked alone".

The royal engagement was officially announced on 24 February and the world was treated to an awkward interview with the couple in which Diana looked obviously besotted with her prince. However, when told by the interviewer that the couple looked very much in love, Charles threw a damper on proceedings by replying "Whatever 'in love' means", a comment that visibly upset Diana.

That evening, Diana moved into Clarence House, the London home of the Queen Mother, as it was obvious that her flat in Chelsea, which she shared with a group of close female friends, was no longer suitable. After dinner that evening she went into the staff quarters, where she proceeded to ride a bicycle around a room chanting "I'm going to

Despite all the tension and drama that had dogged the months before their wedding, Charles and Diana could not have looked happier as they made their way back to Buckingham Palace after the ceremony

Prince Charles & Diana Spencer

Charles and Diana's balcony kiss after the ceremony is one of the most enduring images from the 1981 royal wedding

"DIANA WAS SO NERVOUS THAT SHE GOT CHARLES'S NAME WRONG DURING THE VOWS"

Although most of the official wedding photos were extremely formal, as was traditional at the time, the couple allowed themselves to have some fun with their photographer, Lord Lichfield

marry the Prince of Wales", much to the staff's amusement. Two days later she moved up the road to Buckingham Palace, where she was given a small and rather claustrophobic suite of rooms on the nursery floor.

After spending a number of years sharing the flat her father had bought for her with her friends and being free to come and go as she pleased, this was a depressing experience for Diana, who quickly began to feel bored, lonely and isolated. She spent most of her time alone, as Charles was often away and his family paid her very little attention, assuming that she would quickly adapt to their ways and not realising that she was in desperate need of guidance and support.

Desperate for company, she began to spend time with the palace staff, even holding a small party for them on her 20th birthday, which was a few weeks before her wedding day. While Diana was sequestered in Buckingham Palace, excitement about her forthcoming wedding was reaching fever pitch outside, with souvenirs doing a roaring trade and street parties planned all across the country. There was also a great deal of speculation about Diana's wedding dress, which was being made by a young designer couple, David and Elizabeth Emanuel. It required several fittings and adjustments due to Diana's dramatic weight loss (the result of an eating disorder) during the months before her wedding as she grappled with the pressures of her new position and her growing unease about the close relationship between her fiancé and Camilla Parker Bowles.

When she found out that Charles was planning a private farewell lunch with Mrs Parker Bowles two days before the wedding Diana broke down and even threatened to call off the wedding, only for one of her sisters to point out that it was far too late to pull out as "your face is on the tea towels".

The wedding celebrations began two days before the big day with a final rehearsal in St Paul's Cathedral, which had been chosen as the wedding venue thanks to its enormous size and central location, and then a huge ball held by the Queen in Buckingham Palace, which Diana attended in a daring shocking pink, skin-tight Emanuel gown. Diana spent the night before her wedding at Clarence House with her sisters and bridal attendants, all of whom had to work hard to calm her nerves as she mentally prepared for the biggest day of her life. Prince Charles sent a gift of a signet ring across from Buckingham Palace, accompanied by a note telling her that "I am so proud of you and when you come up I'll be there at the altar for you tomorrow. Just look 'em in the eye and knock them dead." The following morning, 750 million people watched live on television as Diana,

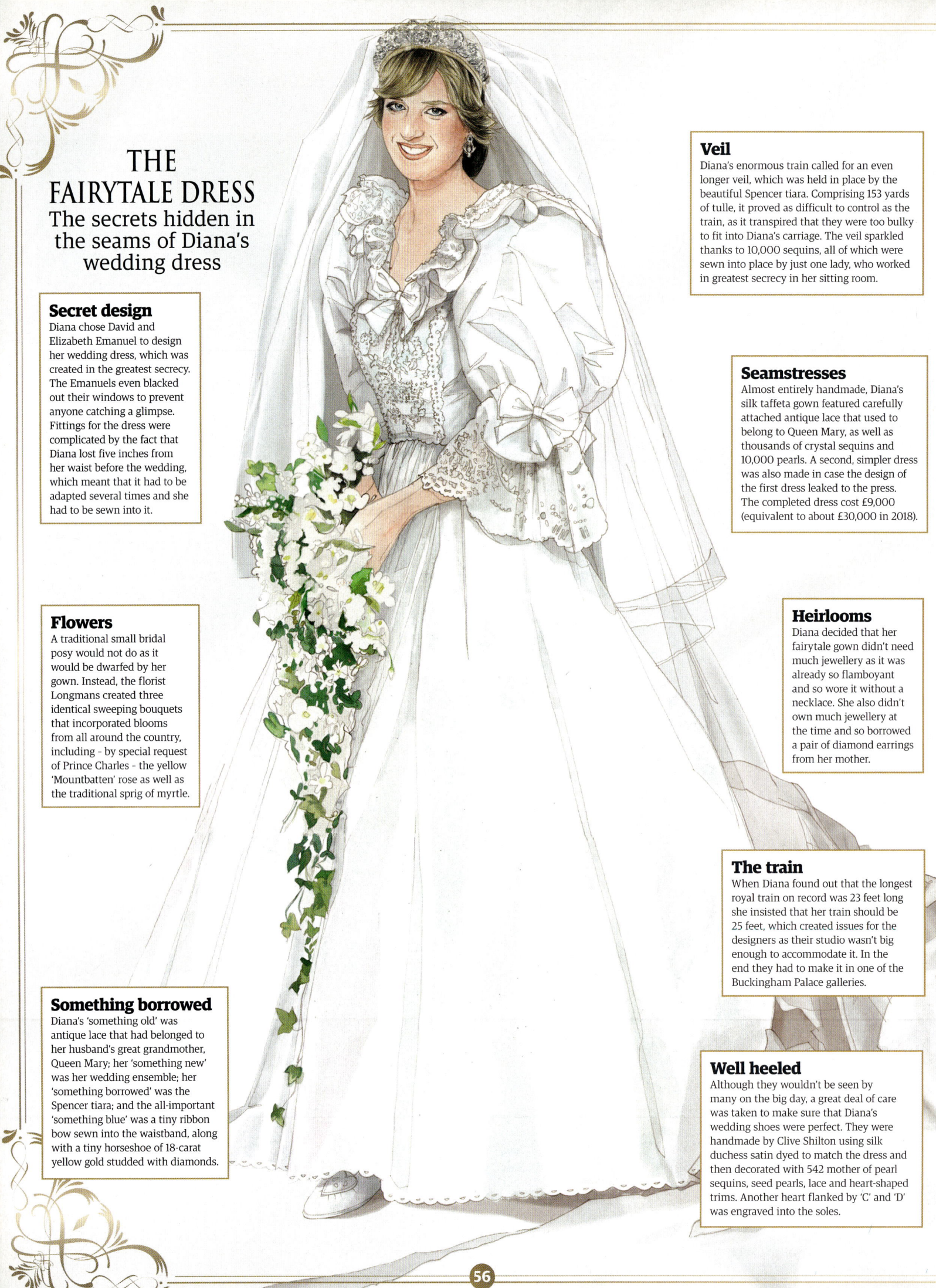

THE FAIRYTALE DRESS
The secrets hidden in the seams of Diana's wedding dress

Secret design
Diana chose David and Elizabeth Emanuel to design her wedding dress, which was created in the greatest secrecy. The Emanuels even blacked out their windows to prevent anyone catching a glimpse. Fittings for the dress were complicated by the fact that Diana lost five inches from her waist before the wedding, which meant that it had to be adapted several times and she had to be sewn into it.

Flowers
A traditional small bridal posy would not do as it would be dwarfed by her gown. Instead, the florist Longmans created three identical sweeping bouquets that incorporated blooms from all around the country, including - by special request of Prince Charles - the yellow 'Mountbatten' rose as well as the traditional sprig of myrtle.

Something borrowed
Diana's 'something old' was antique lace that had belonged to her husband's great grandmother, Queen Mary; her 'something new' was her wedding ensemble; her 'something borrowed' was the Spencer tiara; and the all-important 'something blue' was a tiny ribbon bow sewn into the waistband, along with a tiny horseshoe of 18-carat yellow gold studded with diamonds.

Veil
Diana's enormous train called for an even longer veil, which was held in place by the beautiful Spencer tiara. Comprising 153 yards of tulle, it proved as difficult to control as the train, as it transpired that they were too bulky to fit into Diana's carriage. The veil sparkled thanks to 10,000 sequins, all of which were sewn into place by just one lady, who worked in greatest secrecy in her sitting room.

Seamstresses
Almost entirely handmade, Diana's silk taffeta gown featured carefully attached antique lace that used to belong to Queen Mary, as well as thousands of crystal sequins and 10,000 pearls. A second, simpler dress was also made in case the design of the first dress leaked to the press. The completed dress cost £9,000 (equivalent to about £30,000 in 2018).

Heirlooms
Diana decided that her fairytale gown didn't need much jewellery as it was already so flamboyant and so wore it without a necklace. She also didn't own much jewellery at the time and so borrowed a pair of diamond earrings from her mother.

The train
When Diana found out that the longest royal train on record was 23 feet long she insisted that her train should be 25 feet, which created issues for the designers as their studio wasn't big enough to accommodate it. In the end they had to make it in one of the Buckingham Palace galleries.

Well heeled
Although they wouldn't be seen by many on the big day, a great deal of care was taken to make sure that Diana's wedding shoes were perfect. They were handmade by Clive Shilton using silk duchess satin dyed to match the dress and then decorated with 542 mother of pearl sequins, seed pearls, lace and heart-shaped trims. Another heart flanked by 'C' and 'D' was engraved into the soles.

accompanied by her father Earl Spencer, rode in the famous royal glass coach to St Paul's Cathedral, cheered on by the vast crowds - estimated to be around 650,000 people - that lined the route from Clarence House. There was a loud gasp as she emerged from the carriage and her ivory silk taffeta wedding dress - the subject of months of speculation - was revealed for the first time, sadly crumpled after its long journey squashed into the coach but still beautiful and entirely fitting for a wedding that was being hailed by the public as a real-life fairytale.

The Spencer tiara, a family heirloom that Diana had borrowed for the event, sparkled under the cathedral lights as she made her way slowly up the aisle, past the 3,500 invited guests, her 25-foot train carried behind her by her two youngest bridesmaids. Later on, Diana would recall feeling like "the luckiest girl in the world" to be marrying a man whom she loved so much and that when Charles whispered, "You look beautiful" to her when she reached his side at the altar, she replied, "Beautiful for you."

The couple were married by the archbishop of Canterbury, and although Diana looked extremely poised, she betrayed her nervousness when she got Charles's name wrong during the vows. After the ceremony, the couple returned by carriage to Buckingham Palace, where they posed for the official photographs, which were taken by the Queen's cousin, Lord Lichfield, and enjoyed a lavish wedding breakfast of brill in lobster sauce followed by chicken stuffed with lamb mousse, with strawberries and cream for pudding. There were also no fewer than 27 wedding cakes, including the five-foot-tall official cake, which the couple cut after the ceremony.

For the crowds outside, the next glimpse of the newly married royal couple occurred shortly afterwards when Charles and Diana made the traditional appearance on the Buckingham Palace balcony, flanked by their family and members of the wedding party. Charles had not sealed his wedding vows with a kiss but made up for this oversight by kissing Diana now, creating an iconic image that would feature on dozens of newspapers all around the globe the following day.

According to royal tradition, now a thing of the past, the couple did not stay for the evening party, which was to take place at Claridges, but instead changed into their going-away outfits - in Diana's case, a pretty peach Bellville Sassoon suit with matching hat - then bid their guests goodbye before climbing into the open landau that would take them to Waterloo station.

The groom's mischievous younger brothers, Andrew and Edward, had secretly attached balloons, tin cans and a 'Just Married' sign to the back of the carriage. This delighted the crowds that had gathered to watch the newlyweds leave for their honeymoon, which would involve a few days at Broadlands, Lord Mountbatten's former country home, followed by a Mediterranean cruise on the Royal Yacht Britannia and then several weeks alone on the Balmoral estate.

By the time they returned from honeymoon, Diana's position as an international celebrity, on a scale that had almost certainly never been seen before, had been assured, thanks in part to the romantic magnificence of her wedding day.

That the newly married Prince and Princess of Wales's smiles and happiness masked her secret despair and his growing sense of unease that he had made a terrible mistake in marrying a woman who he did not love with all his heart would not become apparent, to the public at least, for quite some time to come.

While their guests decamped to Claridges for a party, the newly weds headed off on honeymoon - trailed by the balloons attached to their carriage by Charles's brothers

A PRINCE IS BORN

Upon the birth of their first son, Charles and Diana were determined to ensure that he would enjoy as normal an upbringing as possible despite the pressures of royal life and his weighty destiny as future king

The fairytale royal wedding of July 1981, which had captivated millions of viewers, was still fresh in everyone's minds when Charles and Diana visited Wales for three days in October. The couple had been married for just three months, and this was their first tour since their return from honeymoon. Diana, who was secretly battling bulimia as she dealt with the stress of her new role as wife of the heir to the throne, was as beautiful as ever but looked painfully thin as she was greeted by the crowds that had turned out to welcome her to their country. To Diana's dismay, her private battle with depression had recently become exacerbated by tiredness and nausea, which made her life all the more intolerable and made it even harder to maintain a cheerful demeanour in public. It was a relief when she discovered on the second day of the tour that these bouts of debilitating sickness were in fact early symptoms of her first and much-longed-for pregnancy.

As both Charles and Diana adored children and had made no secret of the fact that they were hoping to start a family as soon as possible, they were delighted to learn that they were having a baby so quickly. Although Diana adored her husband and was, like any new wife, keen to have him to herself, she felt desperately lonely and out of place in her new life, finding most of the royal circle intimidatingly chilly and difficult to get along with. A baby would provide her with someone to love and, she hoped, the sort of companionship she was beginning to long for in her isolated private life. Although Charles and Diana ultimately proved to be incompatible, one of the few things that they had in common was the fact they were both struggling to come to terms with their unhappy childhoods - in Diana's case, the divorce of her parents, which had led to feelings of unworthiness and abandonment, while Charles struggled with similar feelings of inadequacy, the result of his strict upbringing and distant relationship with his parents. Both had grown up longing to experience a normal, warm, happy family life and hoped that having children of their own would go some way towards healing the painful wounds of the past.

Like a lot of new parents, the couple kept their news to themselves for almost a month until they were at the stage, around 12 weeks, when the risk of miscarriage significantly diminishes. They couldn't stop the press speculating that there might be a new royal baby on the way though, and the rumours were naturally inflamed by Diana's wan appearance. The Palace chose the day that photos of the princess fast asleep in her chair at a reception appeared in newspapers to announce that Diana was indeed pregnant and that both families were delighted by the news. Previous announcements of royal pregnancies had been formal to the point of evasiveness, whereas this latest announcement was indicative of an increasingly open and communicative attitude on the part of the royal family and also an acknowledgement of Diana's rapport with the British public. Certainly, the news of this particular royal baby was greeted with almost universal delight and regarded by many as a beacon of light for a country in the grip of recession.

Although Diana had been assured that her morning sickness would eventually fade away as the months passed, it actually lingered for the rest of her pregnancy, putting even more stress on the already beleaguered royal marriage. Her husband's friendship with Camilla Parker Bowles was a source of concern to Diana, who suspected that the couple were seeing each other behind her

Prince William was adored by both of his parents, who saw his birth as a chance to lay to rest the ghosts of their own unhappy childhoods and create the perfect, happy family life that they had both desperately longed for

This photo of an exhausted Diana asleep at a function at the Victoria and Albert Museum appeared in newspapers on the same day that the Palace announced her pregnancy with William

"THE PRINCESS IS WELL AND THE BABY'S LOOKING LOVELY. IT'S MARVELLOUS, HE'S NOT BAD"

back. Meanwhile, her pregnancy had not improved relations with her royal in-laws, who remained as distant and, she believed, unfriendly as ever. Diana was just 20 and did not enjoy being surrounded by her husband's much older relations and their staff, most of whom were at least a decade or more older than herself and who had as little time for her as she had for them. She found herself bored by her husband's interests and desperately missed her old life, sharing a flat near Sloane Square with school friends, being squired to parties by eligible young men and enjoying giggly dinner parties.

Matters reached a head during the Christmas visit to Sandringham, when Diana took a tumble down the stairs, landing at the feet of the Queen Mother. Much later, when her marriage was over, she would embellish this incident to make it less an accident than a deliberate, desperate cry for help. According to Diana's version, her husband and his family showed barely any concern for the welfare of either herself or her child, whereas in reality everyone, especially Charles, was extremely worried until a doctor had confirmed that no harm had been done.

The rest of Diana's pregnancy passed without incident until a few days before her due date, when she went into labour and was whisked off to a private room in the Lindo Wing of St Mary's Hospital in Paddington at 5am, with Prince Charles at her side. As many first babies tend to arrive late, Diana had hoped that her child might be born on her own birthday, 1 July, but her son clearly had other ideas and made his appearance to the world at 9.03pm on 21 June, weighing a healthy 7lb ½oz.

The princess was in labour for 16 gruelling hours, supported throughout by her nervous husband, the first royal father to be present at the birth of his child, while the Queen's own gynaecologist, George Pinker, who had looked after Diana during her pregnancy, presided over her labour to ensure a safe delivery for both mother and baby.

Diana was keen to try the natural childbirth techniques that were gaining popularity in the early 1980s and opted for an 'active' labour, during which she stayed as upright as possible, leaning on her husband during contractions and eventually giving birth standing up. Due to the slow and exhausting progress of her labour she was offered medical intervention but, determined to do everything as naturally as possible, she refused. A huge crowd gathered outside the hospital when news of the princess's labour spread, and when Charles – grinning with delight – eventually emerged he was besieged with shouts of congratulations and questions about the baby. The famously reticent Charles was unusually forthcoming at this moment, and informed the well wishers that, "I was immensely relieved when it was all over. The princess is well and the baby's looking lovely. It's marvellous, he's not bad."

The crowds were even larger when the new baby prince, safely cradled in his mother's arms, made his public debut the following day before heading home to the couple's apartment in Kensington Palace, where Princess Margaret had organised a welcome reception for them. The news of his birth had been announced to an overjoyed nation the previous evening by means of the traditional handwritten notice placed on an easel outside Buckingham Palace and, less formally, a

A prince is born

banner across the bottom of television screens all across the country, interrupting a World Cup match. There was immediate speculation about what name would be chosen for the new prince, who had been referred to simply as 'Baby Wales' in hospital, with George being the even-money favourite at bookmakers William Hill. Charles teasingly informed the press that there were two main contenders for the new prince's name, but it would be exactly a week before Buckingham Palace announced that he was to be called William Arthur Philip Louis of Wales. The name William was

enjoying something of a resurgence in popularity at the time but also had the additional bonus of having a royal provenance. Arthur had a similarly medieval resonance and regal providence, while his other names were tributes to his grandfather, Philip, and his father's beloved great uncle Louis, Earl Mountbatten of Burma.

Prince William was baptised on 4 August 1982, the 82nd birthday of his great grandmother, the Queen Mother, in the music room of Buckingham Palace by Robert Runcie, Archbishop of Canterbury. His godparents were King Constantine II of the Hellenes, Lord Romsey, Sir Laurens van der Post, Princess Alexandra, the Duchess of Westminster and Lady Susan Hussey. The baby wore the beautiful Spitalfields silk and Honiton lace christening robe that had been commissioned by Queen Victoria for her eldest daughter in 1841 and then worn by every royal baby until the Queen commissioned a replica in 2008. The Princess of Wales was smiling and radiant in bright pink, which she wore with the diamond and pearl necklace that her husband had given her after William's birth but told friends later that she had felt overwhelmed and was in tears for most of the day.

Although delighted to be a mother, she was suffering from postnatal depression and anxious about her marriage, which was not the great romance that she had anticipated. Life with her baby was certainly not a disappointment though, and she thoroughly enjoyed the time that she spent in the nursery, either at Kensington Palace or their country residence, Highgrove, in Wiltshire. The baby prince had a full-time nanny, Barbara 'Baba' Barnes, but like most royal mothers, Diana insisted upon breast-feeding her baby herself for several months and, along with Charles, took great pride in doing as much as possible for him, although she had to grudgingly accept that her royal duties meant she was unable to spend as much time as she would have liked with her baby.

Diana had barely known Charles before their marriage, and although she was still desperate for his approval, she was also becoming increasingly disenchanted as it became more obvious that they had very little in common. He was 13 years older, set in his ways and could be extremely dull company. Much of this was down to personality, but Diana laid the blame squarely at the feet of his parents and was determined that she would not make the same mistakes with her own children. She saw herself as a royal rebel, forcing the stuffy establishment to become more modern and accessible, especially when it came to the

Crowds gathered together, eager to catch a first glimpse of the new prince

upbringing of her children, whom she wanted to raise as normally as possible without any repressive stuffiness. Diana refurbished both of their homes to make them more comfortable, informal and modern, with particular attention paid to the rooms inhabited by the baby prince, which were filled with colour and stimulating toys and books. Before she married, Diana had loved working as a nanny and kindergarten teacher, and she had very definite ideas about how she wanted her son to be raised. It seemed to her that her husband's upbringing had been rather sad and lonely as his rank had precluded him from making many friends, and he had certainly never been allowed to befriend anyone outside a small, very tight-knit royal circle or have much contact with people from different backgrounds. Diana was determined that William would be raised very differently.

Even the occasional photo calls granted to the press were of a markedly less formal flavour than those of bygone days when royal children would pose stiffly before the cameras, barely bothering to conceal their discomfort and boredom. Instead, Diana would invite her favourite photographers to take photos of the family playing together. The results were warm, informal and affectionate and made the Wales family appear approachable and just like any other couple with a lively baby. One of the most important photo shoots took place during the family's tour of Australia and New Zealand in spring 1983, when William was nine months old. It was the first time that a royal baby had accompanied their parents on tour, the presence of small children having previously been considered too distracting and inconvenient. The Queen and Prince Philip had always left their children behind when embarking on state visits, but Diana, as always, was determined to do things her own way and insisted that William was too young to be left behind for six weeks. Although there were scheduled opportunities for the press and public to catch a glimpse of the little prince, he spent the majority of his time staying on a sheep station in Woomargama in New South Wales with his devoted nanny Baba Barnes in attendance and frequent visits from his parents in between their official engagements.

This trip to Australia underlined the fact that from now on Charles, Diana and their son were to be regarded as a team, a solid family unit, and that unlike the royal children of the past, who had been cared for solely by nannies and saw their parents for only a few minutes every day at teatime, William was being raised as a modern prince and was part of a normal, happy family. However, behind the perfect facade, all was not well in the Wales household, and despite the fact that the couple had expressed a wish to add to their family as quickly as possible, it was to be 18 months before they announced that another royal baby was on its way and that Prince William would no longer be the sole resident of the royal nursery.

Keen to present an informal, approachable image, Diana encouraged the press to take more candid photographs of her family playing together and having fun

A prince is born

"THIS TRIP TO AUSTRALIA UNDERLINED THE FACT THAT FROM NOW ON CHARLES, DIANA AND THEIR SON WERE TO BE REGARDED AS A TEAM"

As one of the most famous children in the world, William quickly developed a complicated and not altogether happy relationship with the press - as this photograph shows

Prince Harry's arrival brought some much-needed happiness to the royal marriage. However, although both of his parents had previously talked about wanting more children, he proved to be their final baby

HURRAH FOR HENRY

An unexpected pregnancy in 1984 brought the ill-matched royal couple closer together than ever before, but these heady days weren't to last.

Diana described the period between the birth of her two sons as "total darkness" due to her deep unhappiness and struggles with bulimia and postnatal depression. Her relationship with her husband had never been easy, but now it was seriously floundering, with very little affection and physical intimacy. The conception of Prince Harry, which probably occurred when the couple were at Sandringham for the traditional royal Christmas gathering, therefore came as something of a surprise, with Diana later referring to it as a miracle. However, although this unexpected event had the potential to put further pressure on the beleaguered royal marriage, instead it brought the two parents closer together.

The pregnancy was announced on Valentine's Day 1984, with the Palace adding that Diana would be continuing her royal duties until August. Much to her relief, the terrible morning sickness that had made her first pregnancy so miserable was not quite so bad this time and eventually faded away. As the pregnancy progressed, her glowing, healthy appearance was much admired. Like many pregnant women, Diana was well aware that people couldn't help staring at her growing bump, and so she dressed with particular care during her pregnancies, favouring pastel, smock dresses, shimmering, loose-fitting evening gowns, and cosy swing coats. However, although Diana was more radiantly beautiful than ever, the old insecurities about her appearance still lingered, and on at least one occasion she broke down in tears during a fitting with the designer Jasper Conran and begged him to make her look 'sexy' for her husband. While she had been wracked with bulimia during her first pregnancy, this time she maintained her ideal weight with a healthy diet and plenty of exercise - habits that would continue for the rest of her life.

Nonetheless, Diana would later remember that she and Charles were "very, very close to each other the six weeks before Harry was born, the closest we've ever, ever been and ever will be". She still suspected that he had resumed his relationship with Camilla Parker Bowles, but for now at least she seemed to have his full attention for once, and she revelled in it. It was not all perfect though - Charles made no secret of his desire to have a daughter, but Diana had discovered during one of her routine ultrasound scans that the new baby was in fact another boy. Unwilling to rock the boat now that things were going well with Charles, she decided to keep this fact to herself and perhaps even deceived him a little as she reportedly bought sets of towels in both pink and blue for the nursery, while the new crib was bedecked with pink ribbons.

The couple were at Windsor Castle when Diana went into labour a week early on the morning of 15 September 1984. They immediately travelled together back to London, accompanied by a police escort. Once again, Diana had decided to give birth in the same room in the Lindo Wing of St Mary's Hospital that Prince William had been born in, rather than labouring at home like most members of the royal family. William had been the first heir to the throne born in hospital, and the experience had been reassuring and pleasant enough that Diana was more than happy to repeat it. Her labour lasted for nine hours and, in line with the rest of the pregnancy, was a much less stressful affair than her previous one. In fact, Diana whiled away most of the time reading a book and dozing in between labour pains. She eventually gave birth, without any pain relief, to a healthy baby boy, weighing 6lb 11oz, at 4.20pm, with Charles at her side. According to Diana, Charles didn't even try to hide his dismay upon learning that the new baby was not just a boy but had also been born with the red hair that had been a trait of the Spencer family for generations. However,

Charles admitted he had wanted his second child to be a girl but was thrilled when his second son was born

"WILLIAM WAS DELIGHTED WITH THE NEW BABY AND INSISTED UPON HOLDING HIS HAND AND KISSING HIM"

Charles seemed thoroughly delighted by his new son when he finally emerged from the hospital doors a couple of hours later and informed the crowd that the baby was "absolutely marvellous," adding for good measure that "it didn't matter if it was a boy or a girl".

The following morning, Charles returned to the hospital, this time accompanied by Prince William, who was to meet his brother for the first time. Although certainly not spoilt by his royal position, the little prince was secure in his hitherto unchallenged position as king of the nursery, and no one was quite sure how he would react to the new rival for his parents' affection. Aware of this, Diana greeted him in the doorway as he ran to her room and hugged him before gently leading him inside. The couple need not have worried - William was delighted with the new baby and insisted upon holding his hand and kissing him. In fact, the expected resentment never came, and both parents would later comment on how much William adored Harry and how he loved to climb into his cot to be with him.

To Diana, who still - even after more than three years of marriage - felt incredibly isolated and lonely within royal circles, this closeness must have been extremely reassuring, as she at least knew that the young siblings would always have someone else to count on in the strange world that they had been born into.

Diana left the hospital a couple of hours later, looking radiant as she emerged from the entrance, holding her baby in the crook of her arm. When Prince William was born she had seemed shy and rather frightened, but this time she was clearly more experienced and confident. This was also reflected in her choice of clothes - with William she had worn the green-and-white polka-dot maternity dress she had worn to go into hospital, while this time she wore a red and white suit and had clearly had her hair freshly coiffured for the occasion. As with William, she opted to breast-feed for as long as possible and take as much practical care of her baby as she could before royal duties took her away. William's beloved nanny, Barbara Barnes, still ultimately presided over the nursery though, assisted by her deputy, Olga Powell.

As with William, the arrival of Prince Henry Charles Albert David of Wales (always to be known from then on as Prince Harry) was heralded with all of the usual pomp and ceremony - two 41-gun salutes fired simultaneously in Hyde Park and the Tower of London; an official written announcement of his birth propped on an easel outside Buckingham Palace; and eventually, a grand christening dressed in the Victorian lace christening gown that had been worn by six generations of royal babies.

The christening was performed in St George's Chapel in Windsor Castle by the Archbishop of Canterbury. Harry's godmothers were Lady Sarah Armstrong-Jones (his father's cousin), Carolyn Bartholomew (his mother's friend and former flatmate), and Lady Celia Vestey (the Queen's close friend). Harry's godfathers were Prince Andrew (his uncle) and artist Bryan Organ and stockbroker Gerald Ward (his father's friends).

Hurrah for Henry

The reception afterwards was a relaxed and happy affair, as evidenced by the footage filmed for the Queen's Christmas speech a few days later. Prince William was clearly determined to be the centre of attention, which made everyone laugh, with the exception of his great-uncle, Lord Snowdon, who was taking the official photographs and found his young nephew's larks immensely trying.

Overall though, Harry's birth was regarded as a harbinger of better times to come for both his family and the nation as a whole, with his grandmother taking time in her Christmas speech to remark upon how, "The happy arrival of our fourth grandchild gave great cause for family celebrations. But for parents and grandparents, a birth is also a time for reflection on what the future holds for the baby and how they can best ensure its safety and happiness. To do that, I believe we must be prepared to learn as much from them as they do from us.

"We could use some of that sturdy confidence and devastating honesty with which children rescue us from self doubts and self delusions. We could borrow that unstinting trust of the child in its parents for our dealings with each other."

Charles, Diana, Prince William and Prince Harry look out from the deck of the Royal Yacht Britannia in Venice, Italy, in May 1985

Always keen to be the centre of attention, Prince William's antics at his brother's christening amused his relatives but not the photographer

ON THE ROCKS

Charles and Diana were once a fairytale couple, yet over the years their seemingly perfect marriage fell apart long before they reached their happy ever after

Words **Catherine Curzon**

The couple's mutual dislike was evident on their 1992 tour of India

On the rocks

When Diana was photographed alone at the Taj Mahal it sent a clear message to the public

Charles, Prince of Wales, and Lady Diana Spencer met in late 1977, when Diana was just 16 and Charles was nearing his 30th birthday. He was dating Diana's older sister at the time and had no romantic interest in the younger woman, but eventually they were to become one of the most famous and controversial couples that the world had ever known. When Charles and Diana met again three years later at a polo match, their circumstances had changed. She was older and he was single. It was the start of a romance that would rock the royal family.

Charles and Diana were engaged in early 1981 and their marriage that summer was watched by a staggering 750 million people worldwide. It seemed like the perfect fairytale, and when Prince William was born the following year the nation was sure that all was rosy indeed between the Prince and Princess of Wales. In fact, they couldn't have been more wrong. The marriage of the heir to the throne and his young bride was already in crisis, and over the coming years things would get a whole lot worse.

Both Charles and Diana had experienced doubts on the eve of their wedding but had gone ahead with the ceremony thanks to the sheer weight of expectation and fear of what might happen if they didn't. The cracks began to show on their honeymoon, and in 1982, while pregnant with William, Diana allegedly threw herself down a staircase during a period of depression. For the first few years of their marriage the couple attempted to overcome their differences, but after the birth of Prince Harry the cracks between the Prince and Princess of Wales widened into a chasm and both husband and wife embarked on affairs.

Charles turned to Camilla Parker Bowles, who had been his girlfriend years earlier and had remained a close friend. Diana, meanwhile, began a passionate affair with Major James Hewitt, who had taught her sons to ride. Though Harry was born years before the affair began, that didn't stop the press from speculating that Hewitt and Harry, who were both redheads, were father and son. It is an allegation that Hewitt has always denied.

One of the most famous and enduring images capturing the end of the royal marriage came in 1992, when Charles and Diana visited India together. 12 years earlier Charles had been pictured sitting alone on a bench in front of the Taj Mahal, and now Diana recreated the image, cutting a poignant and rather lonely figure as her husband accompanied British representatives on a trip to Bangalore. The picture hit the front pages and with it the public saw the very first and very public indication that things were not going well for the Prince and Princess of Wales. Though Charles's excursion had been planned weeks previously, the British public interpreted his absence as one borne out of spite, as though he had abandoned Diana to make the trip alone. The symbolism of the venue, built to honour a loved and missed wife by her grieving husband, wasn't lost on them either. Just a few days later those suspicions were compounded when the couple attended a polo match during the same trip. When Charles moved closer for a kiss, Diana pointedly turned her head away.

It was only the tip of how bad things had become for the couple. In 1989 Diana made a public scene when she confronted Camilla about her

"IT WAS LIKE NOTHING THE ROYAL FAMILY HAD BEEN SUBJECTED TO BEFORE"

Princess in Love turned the breakdown of the royal marriage into a soap opera

PRINCESS IN LOVE
When the Prince and Princess of Wales split, their marriage became soap opera fodder

In 1994, James Hewitt contacted journalist Anna Pasternak and asked if she would be interested in negotiating a deal for the story of his relationship with Princess Diana. Hewitt regularly played polo with Prince Charles and had been employed to help Diana and her sons improve their equestrian skills, a role that eventually led to their affair. He told Pasternak that he was smuggled into Kensington Palace in the boot of a car and that he had supported Diana through her battle with bulimia, becoming an indispensable prop to the troubled princess until he was posted overseas thanks to meddling senior royals.

Pasternak's subsequent book, *Princess in Love*, was a worldwide cause celebre. It sold hundreds of thousands of copies and was adapted into an American television movie that reimagined the affair as a tragic romance in the grand tradition of daytime soap operas, complete with a dashing hero, a tragic heroine and anonymous country house hotels standing in for Highgrove and Balmoral. It wasn't the first nor the last time that the Prince and Princess of Wales would become the stars of prime-time fiction. While their romance might have seemed like a fairytale, their split was pure melodrama.

affair with Charles at a birthday party for Camilla's sister, and that explosive allegation reached an enormous audience in 1992 with the publication of Andrew Morton's scandalous bestseller, *Diana: Her True Story*. Following hot on the heels of the book came a series of ever-more damaging and explicit newspaper revelations that shook the royal family to its core. *The Sun* publicised the existence of tape recordings between Diana and her close friend James Gilbey in which he affectionately referred to her as 'Squidgy'. When the tabloid made the audio available on a premium rate number, Diana called the hotline to listen. She little suspected what was to follow just a few months later.

In November 1992, the 'Camillagate' tapes eclipsed anything that 'Squidgygate' could offer as Charles regaled Camilla Parker Bowles with his fantasies of being reincarnated as her underwear or even a tampon. It was like nothing the royal family had been subjected to before and for weeks the front pages were filled with ever-more explicit revelations. Behind closed doors the Queen and the Duke of Edinburgh did what they could to reconcile the pair, but it was too late to turn back.

As the Prince and Princess of Wales battled it out at home, Highgrove split into two halves in what became known as the 'War of the Waleses'. On one side were the loyal staff of Charles, and on the other those close to Diana. It led to a tense and sometimes explosive atmosphere, which household servants such as Paul Burrell, Diana's former butler, were later to discuss at great length in the press. Long-time colleagues became enemies as the court divided, with an atmosphere of malign suspicion dominating a world in which both camps were on the lookout for spies. Between the prince and princess, meanwhile, things became increasingly strained. They reached a head, Burrell claimed, when the usually placid Charles confronted him in the library at Highgrove and accused him of spying on behalf of Diana. When Burrell protested his innocence, Charles threw a heavy book at him and demanded that he never discuss the life of the prince with his estranged wife.

Burrell, of course, hitched his wagon firmly to the Princess of Wales, and as things at Highgrove reached boiling point, she left Highgrove to take up residence in Kensington Palace with Burrell at her side. As the royal households reshuffled, both Charles and Diana tried to position themselves to command both the most influential and useful staff and the upper hand. The split was therefore rancourous, with locks changed and walkouts for some, while others rose in the pecking order seemingly overnight.

Diana in particular looked to form enduring and sometimes very personal relationships with those who left Highgrove with her. Sometimes

Diana's affair with James Hewitt led to baseless rumours over the paternity of one of her sons

On the rocks

these relationships ended badly, such as when her private secretary resigned in the wake of her *Panorama* interview, while in other cases staff who had initially pledged their loyalty to Diana realised they had made a mistake once they arrived at Kensington Palace. When Diana heard that her chauffeur was leaving her household to return to Charles's side she was utterly devastated. She reportedly delayed her confirmed appearance at a public engagement to flee from her car into Hyde Park, where she wept bitterly at the perceived betrayal.

One of the most controversial figures who remained loyal to Charles was Tiggy Legge-Bourke, who became a close friend to the young princes. Diana was deeply jealous of their relationship and an altercation between the two women at a Christmas party resulted in Legge-Bourke threatening to take legal action against the princess. The split could not have been more acrimonious.

In December 1992, Prime Minister John Major stood up in the House of Commons and announced the separation of the Prince and Princess of Wales to the nation. Though he claimed that it was amicable, in fact it was anything but. Diana went on a press offensive, capitalising on the widespread public support that she had gained in the wake of the split. If there had been any hopes of a reconciliation, they were blown out of the water by the princess's infamous tell-all *Panorama* interview.

It was the final straw. 12 months after the couple had parted, Charles and Diana began the proceedings that would lead to their divorce. For the Prince and Princess of Wales, the fairytale had ended with a bump.

Before long Charles's old flame Camilla Parker Bowles was attracting press attention

Lady Diana Spencer was a nursery teacher whose sister was one of Charles's close friends

THE END OF A FAIRYTALE

Charles and Diana's marriage had been on the rocks for over a decade, but matters reached a scandalous head when they separated in 1992 after a series of scurrilous headlines

On 9 December 1992, the world was astounded when the British Prime Minister John Major stood up in the House of Commons and announced that the Prince and Princess of Wales had decided to separate, adding that it was amicable, they had no plans to divorce, and that there was every chance that Diana might still be crowned queen one day. There had been rumours that Charles and Diana's marriage was on the rocks for nearly a decade, but even so, this stark, official announcement took almost everyone by surprise. While the country and international press dissected this unexpected turn of events and speculated about what precisely had gone wrong between the royal couple, Charles and Diana were, like all newly separated couples, privately working out the minutiae of their new lives - in particular the arrangements for their beloved boys. It was immediately announced that while Charles would now be dividing his time between Highgrove and Clarence House, Diana would be remaining in their apartment in Kensington Palace, and that the boys would be dividing their time between them when they weren't at school, with both parents equally responsible for their upbringing.

Ten-year-old William and eight-year-old Harry had been aware for quite some time that their parents' marriage was failing - it would have been impossible not to notice the growing air of tension between Charles and Diana as they led increasingly separate lives and spent as little time as possible in each other's company. Even so, the news of their separation, which was gently broken to them in private, hit them both very hard.

The royal family, in particular their grandparents, the Queen and Prince Philip, now rallied around to make sure that they felt fully loved and supported at this difficult time, which was made all the more onerous by all of the public attention now trained upon them.

In some ways, though, it must have been a relief - their mother was often miserable and in tears and would even later on recall her eldest son passing tissues to her under a bathroom door and begging her not to cry as she sobbed helplessly on the other side. After the separation, both parents became visibly happier, and as a consequence the princes, too, felt the mood lighten at home. Despite this, it was tough to go to school knowing that their classmates and teachers knew all about their parents' private affairs. In particular, for William, the sensitive and reserved elder boy who already deeply resented the relentless press intrusion into their lives, it was especially painful.

Rumours that both Charles and Diana had indulged in extramarital affairs had persisted throughout 1992 - fuelled first by the publication of Andrew Morton's explosive and scandalous biography of Diana. It was revealed after her death that it had been written with her full assistance and based on lengthy recorded interviews, during which she unburdened herself of years of unhappiness and frustration about her hostile husband, his unsupportive family and the omnipresent Camilla Parker Bowles. Following this was the so-called 'Squidgygate' tape of the princess, the eponymous 'Squidgy' enjoying an intimate chat with a male friend who was later revealed to be debonaire man-about-town James Gilby. *The Sun* broke the story on its front page in August with the headline 'MY LIFE IS TORTURE' and even set up a phone line that would enable the curious to listen to the actual recording. It was one of the final blows to the floundering royal marriage, and worse was to come in January 1993 when the *Daily Mirror* published the transcript of a private and clearly sexually charged conversation between Charles and his lover Camilla Parker Bowles.

All of this was deeply embarrassing for the adults concerned, but for their children it was thoroughly humiliating. Naturally, their immediate circle did everything they could to protect the boys from the scandal and rumours, but it proved impossible to keep it entirely at bay, especially now that they were both at school and

Towards the end of their relationship, it became harder for Charles and Diana to hide their feelings, as is evident in this photo, taken on their trip to South Korea

"THE ALWAYS DEEPLY INSECURE DIANA RELIED HEAVILY ON HER SONS FOR SUPPORT"

associating with people outside the royal family circle. Their parents did all they could to make life easier for them, but as tensions rose between the two rival households, with both Charles and Diana determined to garner the most sympathy and positive press attention, it became increasingly difficult to shield the princes from the effects of their parents' actions, as more photographers than ever hounded them, and the stories swirling around the royal couple became more lurid.

From now on, their time was divided between Charles at Highgrove and their mother at Kensington Palace, with all of the usual annual royal events at Sandringham, Buckingham Palace and Balmoral in between. Harry would later remember that he and his brother spent a lot of time "bouncing between the two of them" in the backs of cars (and having play fights that he would always win) and feeling like they never saw quite enough of either parent - a common complaint among children of separated parents, who feel themselves divided in two and are often called upon to take sides.

However, although Diana had always been the more visibly affectionate and fun parent and might well have expected to have their loyalty, it could be said that Charles came into his own as a father after the separation and that ultimately the boys seemed equally happy with both. All of their usual holidays continued - to Klosters, Spain and Barbados - but now they were accompanied by only one of their parents. Worried that they might be in need of company, Charles hired a family friend, Tiggy Legge-Bourke, to act as nanny and companion to the boys while they were living with him. Well connected, fun-loving and extremely fond of outdoor pursuits like skiing, hunting and shooting, Tiggy fitted into the royal circles and was adored by her charges - much to the jealous annoyance of their mother, who loathed Legge-Bourke and would later put it about that not only was she sleeping with Charles with an eye to becoming his second wife but that she'd had a pregnancy terminated as a result. Like a lot of separated mothers, the always deeply insecure Diana relied heavily on her sons for emotional support and resented the constant presence of another woman in their lives.

Privately, the war between the Waleses continued to escalate, and when Diana seemed to have gained the upper hand by dramatically announcing her retirement from public life, implying that her husband had driven her away, Charles retaliated by working with Jonathan Dimbleby on an authorised biography and accompanying documentary. Intended as a riposte to the damaging allegations about the prince that had appeared in Morton's

The end of a fairytale

Charles hired family friend Tiggy Legge-Bourke to act as nanny and companion to the boys while they were living with him. Tiggy went on various holidays with them

book before the separation, the documentary, which was screened in June 1994, was intended to show a more personable side to Charles. It was an attempt to rehabilitate his reputation in the eyes of a public who seemed to be very much on the side of his estranged wife. However, although the public were indeed won over by the scenes of Charles's domestic life with his sons, they were less impressed by his frank admission that he had indeed been unfaithful to Diana during their marriage. What the two princes thought of this is unknown, but it must have hurt them very much.

However, the furore over Charles's confession was overshadowed two months later when the press revealed Diana's long-term affair with married art dealer Oliver Hoare, whom she had been pestering with anonymous phone calls as he bounced between her and his wife. Worse was to come in October when Anna Pasternak's explosive book, *Princess in Love*, which spilled the beans on Diana's hitherto secret relationship with James Hewitt, was published.

This latter revelation was particularly damaging to her boys as, although the affair had lasted for almost five years, beginning in 1986 and ending in 1990, the similarities between the auburn-haired Hewitt's colouring and that of Prince Harry inevitably gave rise to all manner of unsavoury and completely fabricated conjecture about the true parentage of the young prince – which unfortunately lingers on to this day.

Deeply hurt by Hewitt's betrayal of her trust, wounded by the crude jibes in the press and increasingly feeling isolated and out of place, Diana began to seriously consider leaving Britain and starting again elsewhere, potentially America, where she had always been enormously popular. It was the unwillingness to leave her precious boys that kept her in London though. More than ever, she felt that her most significant duty was to mold William into a very modern future king and provide both boys with as normal an upbringing as possible.

As she felt herself increasingly excluded from royal life, her old resentment of the stuffiness, coldness and hostility of her husband's family and their circle only increased and made her even more determined to make sure that her boys would be completely different. She had always been frustrated by Charles's lack of empathy for ordinary people and so continued the private evening visits to homeless shelters and soup kitchens, where her sons could see for themselves just how their poorest and most vulnerable future subjects lived. Their leisure time became increasingly egalitarian too, with trips to Disney World in Florida and, closer to home, Thorpe Park, where Diana and her boys paid and queued up for the rides alongside everyone else.

After her relationship with Hoare came to an end in 1995, Diana had a short affair with rugby player Will Carling, another married man. When this relationship broke up, she became involved with Pakistani heart surgeon Dr Hasnat Khan, with whom she fell deeply in love. The completely besotted Diana, normally so circumspect when it came to her private affairs, even introduced Khan to her sons, but they were reportedly unimpressed, having much preferred the now disgraced James Hewitt, who had given them riding lessons and been more than happy to talk for hours to the two army-obsessed boys about his time as an officer in the Life Guards. The fact that Diana was seriously contemplating marrying Khan and moving with him to Pakistan probably endeared him even less to the two princes, who already felt like they didn't see enough of their mother - especially now that both were away at boarding school.

Although Diana genuinely felt that her sons were the centre of her world, she seemed blind to the effects that her own poor decisions were having on them at this time. Wounded by the failure of her marriage, suspicious of her husband and his circle and unsure of what her future should hold, she seemed hopelessly adrift and leaned heavily on her sons for emotional support. This desperate need for approval would lead to the infamously candid *Panorama* interview with Martin Bashir that was televised in November 1995 - to the horror of the royals and consternation of the press and 22.8 million members of the public who tuned in to watch. What her sons thought at the time is unknown, but William has since said that he understands why his mother might have felt desperate enough to go public.

Although Diana's *Panorama* interview gained her some public sympathy, the reaction in her immediate circle was less pleasing, and her royal in-laws were horrified. The Queen and Prince Philip, who had weathered many a personal storm during their marriage, were especially wounded by Diana's assertions that she had been effectively abandoned by their family, when in fact both had been very supportive of Diana and tried their best to be understanding of her predicament. Philip was particularly fond of Diana and had even privately written to her to express his support and offer advice, which she was clearly very touched by. This all changed after the *Panorama* broadcast, however, and although the Queen was apparently inclined to be sympathetic to Diana's woes, Philip was furious at what he saw as her betrayal of their family. They were also very concerned about the effect that all this airing of dirty laundry would be having on the two vulnerable young princes. In consequence, on 20 December, shortly after Diana had announced that she would not after all be joining the royal family for their annual Christmas celebration at Sandringham, Buckingham Palace announced that the Queen had written to her son and daughter-in-law to recommend that they divorce.

The official announcement of the couple's divorce came in February 1996, and negotiations for Diana's settlement and arrangements for the princes immediately began in earnest, although nothing would be finally settled until June. In exchange for dropping her title of 'Her Royal Highness', Diana came away with £17.5 million and the right to remain in Kensington Palace with her sons, whom she would still have equal access to when they weren't away at school. It was a rather prosaic end to a marriage that had begun with a fairy-tale wedding almost 15 years earlier, but although it had ended badly, both Charles and Diana would have said it was entirely worth it because of their beloved boys.

Charles and Diana leave the church of St Mary Magdalene near Sandringham House, Christmas Day 1994. It was Diana's last Christmas with the royal family

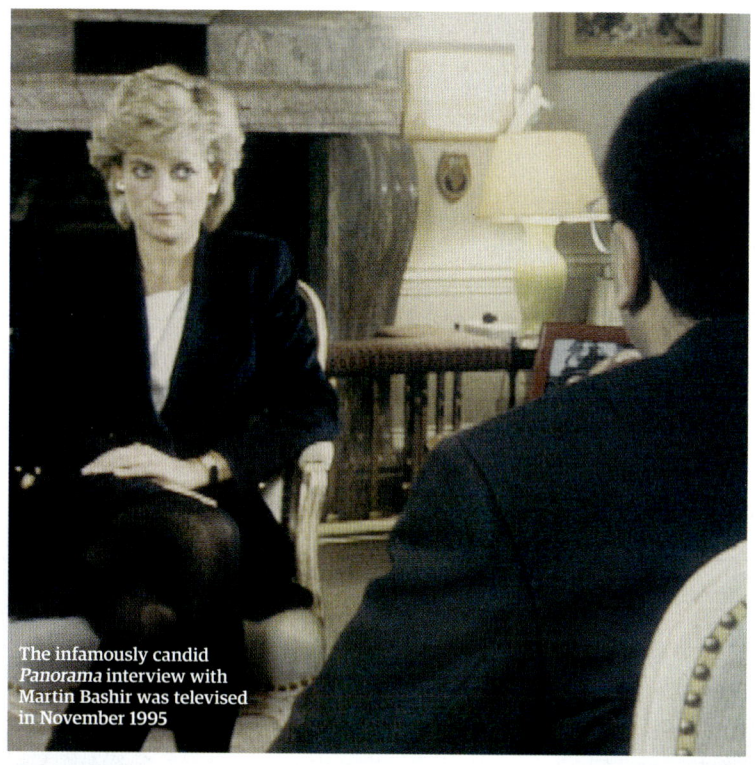

The infamously candid *Panorama* interview with Martin Bashir was televised in November 1995

DAILY STAR
QUEEN TELLS DI TO SPLIT

Daily Express
GENE BREAKTHROUGH IN BATTLE AGAINST BREAST CANCER
JUDGE BACKS RIGHT TO HIT A THUG
Queen orders Diana divorce

THE Sun
Sun World Exclusive
QUEEN ORDERS DIVORCE
Letter tells Di and Charles: End it

TODAY READERS WELCOME TODAY
DAILY Mirror
1,000 knives
AMAZING START TO AMNESTY
QUEEN TELLS CHARLES AND DI TO
WORLD EXCLUSIVE
By THE EDITOR

The Daily Telegraph

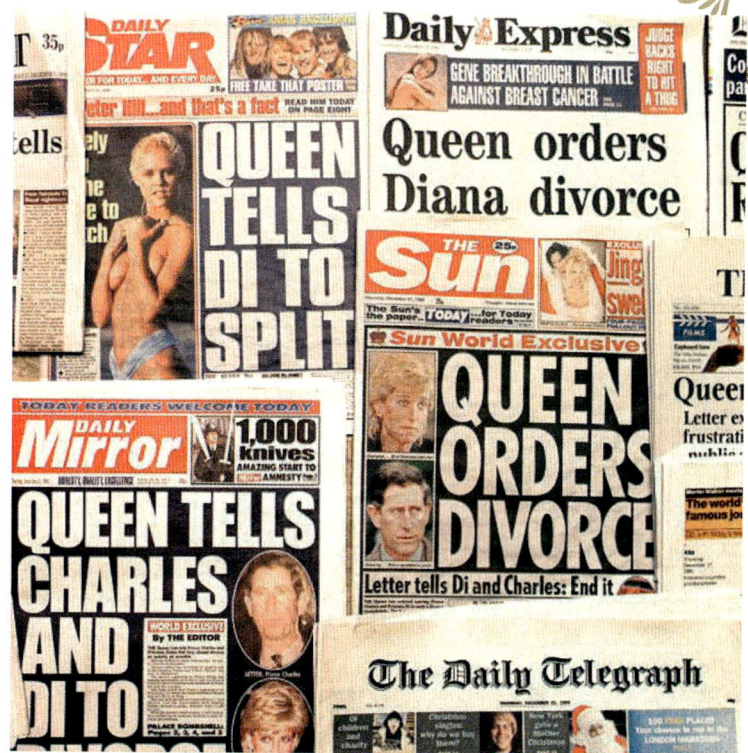

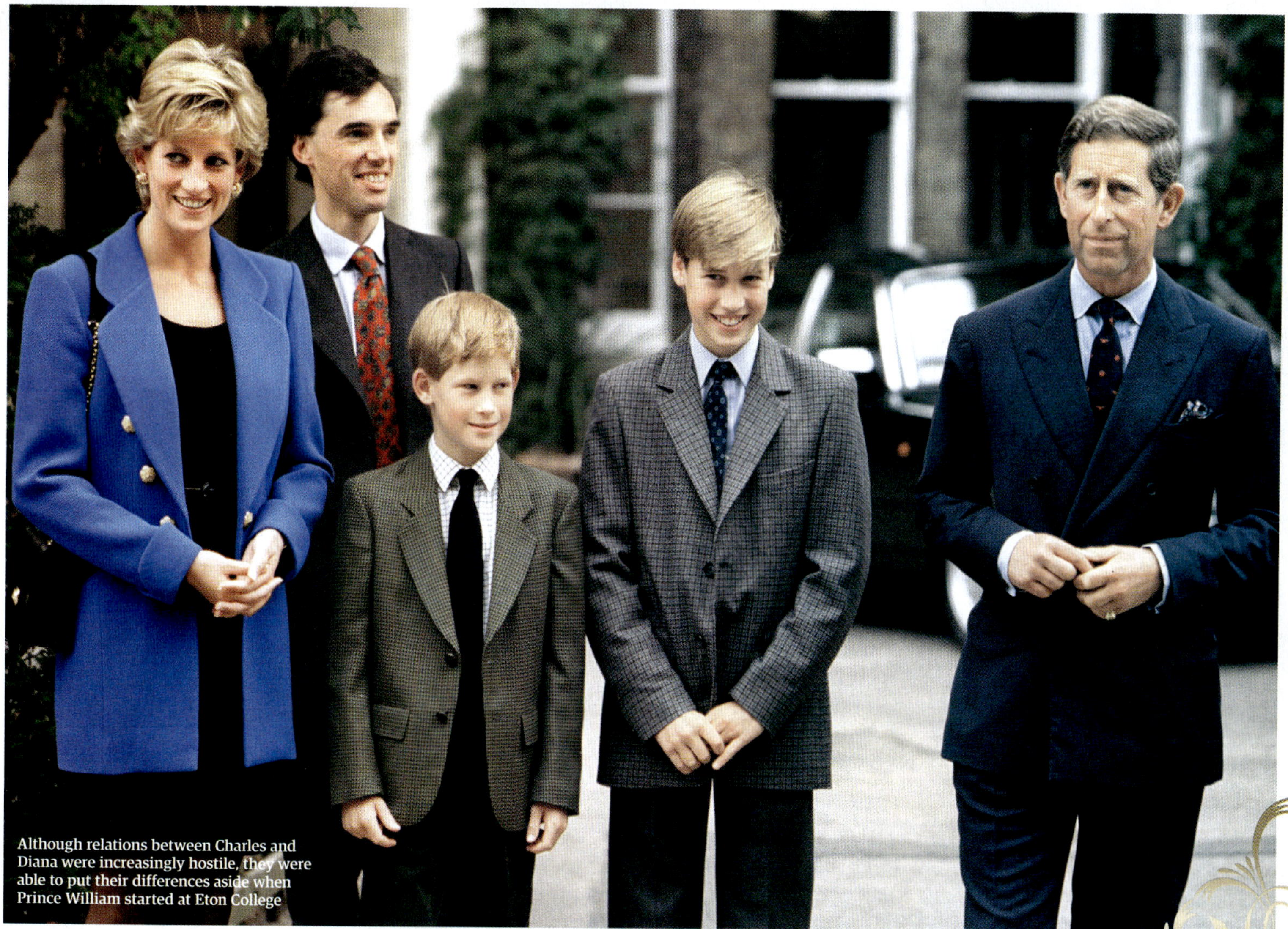

Although relations between Charles and Diana were increasingly hostile, they were able to put their differences aside when Prince William started at Eton College

HEARTACHE & HAPPINESS

80 Death of a princess
A horrendous car crash in the heart of Paris claimed the lives of three people, including the woman hailed as 'the people's princess', and plunged Britain into a period of stunned mourning

88 Single parent
Helping his sons to heal in the wake of their mother's death was a delicate process for Charles

94 Rekindling true love
Two former lovers gave new life to an old flame when Charles and Camilla made their relationship public, but many struggled to forgive their affair so soon after Diana's death

98 The wedding of Charles & Camilla
Inside the wedding that finally joined two kindred spirits in matrimony

DEATH OF A PRINCESS

When it was revealed that the Princess of Wales had tragically died in a car crash in Paris the outpouring of public grief was unprecedented

On 31 August 1997, the country woke up to the shocking news that Diana, Princess of Wales, had died in Paris just hours earlier.

When news of the accident first broke in the UK at around 1am, it was reported that although her companion, Dodi Fayed, had already died, the princess had merely been injured. However, as the hours went on and more news was released it became increasingly clear that the incident had been much more serious than people had realised.

Nonetheless, there was still universal disbelief when newsreader Martyn Lewis, who looked equally shellshocked, opened the BBC One news with the stark announcement that, "Diana, Princess of Wales, has died after a car crash in Paris. The French Government announced her death just before five o'clock this morning. Buckingham Palace confirmed the news shortly afterwards."

Within half an hour, the first bouquet had been placed outside the gates of Kensington Palace - the first of thousands that would arrive over the following days as the public, most of whom had never even met Diana, sought to express their grief and total disbelief that she was gone and that the story that had begun with a fairytale wedding 16 years earlier had now met such a tragic end.

After her divorce was finalised a year earlier in August 1996, Diana had worked extremely hard to find her feet. Although at times she undoubtedly struggled to find purpose in her new life, she had never looked better or more happy. Diana, it seemed, was at last starting to find her place in the world as an ambassadress for her chosen causes, most notably when she travelled to Bosnia and Angola to campaign for the removal of landmines, which even in times of peace continued to kill hundreds of innocent people.

Her tempestuous two-year relationship with cardiologist Hasnat Khan had finally come to an end in June 1997, and shortly afterwards she had frequently been seen in the company of Dodi Fayed, the playboy son of Harrods owner Mohamed Al-Fayed, whom she had met while staying at his father's villa in St Tropez with her sons at the start of July. At the end of the month, William and Harry had joined their father at Balmoral, but they were planning to rejoin their mother on the last day of August before returning to Eton.

Lonely without her boys and both flattered and amused by Dodi's relentless attention, Diana began to spend a lot of time with him, often joining him at the villa in the south of France or on his yacht. Although this rather improbable romance is unlikely to have blossomed into a serious relationship, the world's press obsessed over the pair all summer, featuring photos of Diana and Dodi on front pages and speculating about whether she would convert to Islam in order to marry him.

Among her friends there was some speculation that the whole affair had been manufactured by Diana to make Hasnat Khan jealous while at the same time infuriating her ex-husband and his family. However, what she had failed to consider was what her sons - who didn't particularly like Dodi - might think about her new relationship. William was particularly unimpressed, as he sensed that association with the Fayeds would not do his mother credit and was understandably worried about what the other boys would say about it all when he returned to Eton in the autumn.

Since the break up of his parents' marriage his mercurial mother had increasingly leant upon him for emotional support, relying upon him for both reassurance and advice. It was the belief of her friends that Dodi was on borrowed time from the start, because he wouldn't be around for long once 15-year-old William told her to get rid of him.

At the end of August, Dodi and Diana enjoyed a break in Sardinia on his father's yacht before going to Paris, where they planned to stay in the Fayed-owned Ritz Hotel on the Place Vendôme. After an unsuccessful evening, the pair decided to retreat from the Ritz, where it seemed like every press photographer in all of Paris was lying in wait for them, and instead stay at Dodi's apartment near the Champs-Élysées.

The funeral of Diana, Princess of Wales, was watched by more than a million people on the streets, more than 31 million on television in the UK, and around 2 billion worldwide. For her sons and family it was still an intensely personal event, made all the more difficult by the knowledge that the eyes of the world were on them

They set off at 12.20am in the back of a black Mercedes, which was driven by the Ritz Deputy Head of Security Henri Paul, with bodyguard Trevor Rees-Jones sitting in the passenger seat. Neither Diana nor Dodi were wearing a seat belt, while Paul had spent the evening drinking alcohol in the bar and would later prove to be over the legal driving limit. Diana would never have been allowed to travel in such unsafe conditions in the past, but when she lost her right to be addressed as 'Your Royal Highness' she also gave up her right to a royal security team, who would have prevented her from getting into Dodi's car that fateful evening.

Pursued by a swarm of photographers, the Mercedes sped away from the Ritz, crossed the Place de la Concorde and headed towards the Champs-Élysées. Disaster soon struck after they entered the underpass tunnel by the Pont de l'Alma as Henri lost control of the speeding Mercedes and crashed it into one of the many pillars that lined the tunnel.

When the first of the pursuing paparazzi arrived at the scene just a few moments later they were horrified to discover that the Mercedes was now a mangled mess of metal and that the driver and Dodi Fayed were clearly dead, while bodyguard Rees-Jones had severe injuries to his face. Most attention, however, was on the injured but still conscious Diana, who was crumpled in the back of the vehicle. As they waited for emergency services to arrive some of the photographers tried to help, but others continued to take photographs despite entreaties to stop.

Although it had at first seemed possible that she might survive the catastrophe, once Diana was released from the wreckage it became clear just how serious her injuries were. She suffered a cardiac arrest and required ten minutes of CPR before she was considered stable enough to be moved. Despite the best efforts of French medical staff at the Pitié-Salpêtrière Hospital in Paris, Diana was declared dead at 4am local time.

Several hundred miles away at Balmoral Castle, it was 3am, and the two princes were fast asleep after a busy day playing with their cousins. They had not seen their mother for almost a month but had kept in regular contact, her last brief call having been made from Paris the previous evening. Much later, the two boys would recall cutting the phone call short because they wanted to return to the game they were playing and regretted not having spoken to her for longer.

Their father was informed of the accident at 1am and had anxiously waited for news until confirmation arrived that Diana had died in hospital. Devastated, he spent the next few hours walking around the gardens and worrying about how to tell his children that their mother was dead before finally waking William just after 7am. Together they then went to Harry's room to break the news. Later that Sunday morning the trio, obviously completely

Charles holds the hand of Prince Harry as they view bouquets of flowers left in memory of Diana, Princess of Wales, in September 1997 in Balmoral, Scotland

Death of a princess

"Stop telling us what to do with those boys! You're talking like they're commodities!"

stunned and suffering terribly, accompanied the rest of the royal family to morning service at the local church. Strangely, there was no mention of Diana during the service, which prompted the confused Harry to ask his father if his mother was actually really dead. When Charles made arrangements to travel to Paris in order to bring Diana's body back to London, Harry begged to accompany him but was gently advised to remain at Balmoral with his grandparents.

Although everyone was deeply shocked and distressed by Diana's sudden death, the chief priority of everyone at Balmoral was to ensure that her two anguished sons received as much support as possible.

Their often-irascible grandfather, Prince Philip, was especially supportive of them at this time. He had not been much older than William when he experienced the tragedy of losing his favourite sister, Cecilie, along with her husband and three of their children in a plane crash, and so he had a better idea than most of how they may be feeling.

He took them on several long hikes and stalks through the estate at this time, allowing them to either walk in silence or talk about their feelings. Meanwhile, their grandmother, the Queen, ordered that all newspapers be banned from the castle and that every television and radio be hidden away in order to protect them from the lurid speculations and sensationalism being spread by the press.

Their aunt, Princess Anne, who admittedly had never been very fond of Diana but loved her boys, was also extremely supportive, particularly of Harry, who was clearly struggling and whom she took out on long rides. She also enlisted her children, Zara and Peter, to take the lost, anguished boys under their wings.

However, as the royal family firmly closed ranks to protect and care for the two boys at the very heart of this terrible tragedy, it began to look to the public as though they were actively shunning the huge outpouring of collective grief that had greeted the shocking news of Diana's passing.

Some royal deaths, notably that of the Queen's own father, George VI, had been marked by genuine mourning on the part of the public, but the establishment had never before seen anything on such an enormous scale, and so they underestimated just how seriously it should be taken and miscalculated their response to it. The Queen and Prince Philip were so focused on protecting William and Harry from the spotlight and treating the death of their mother as a private tragedy that they failed to appreciate the feelings of a nation that also felt bereaved.

Only Charles seemed to understand, and he was the driving force behind the family's acknowledgement of Diana's popularity and status in the public sphere. It was he who insisted upon a public funeral at Westminster Abbey when his parents were instead in favour of the Spencer family organising a private ceremony.

Family discussions about the funeral naturally involved some talk of the role that the two princes should play, and at one point an enraged Prince Philip burst out, "Stop telling us what to do with those boys! They've lost their mother and you're talking about them as though they're commodities! Have you any idea what they're going through?" At

Although the Queen and the Spencer family had wanted the funeral to be a private affair, Prince Charles believed that the public needed a more official send-off at Westminster Abbey

After returning to London, the princes and their father took the time to survey the sea of flowers that had surrounded Kensington Palace since Diana's death

The images of the young princes following Diana's coffin shocked and moved the public and remain an enduring testament to the love they had for their mother

Death of a princess

another time, he interrupted a discussion to say that the most pressing matter on his mind was the fact that William had run away somewhere on the Balmoral estate and couldn't be found.

Meanwhile, the press continued to condemn the royal family's lack of visibility, which prompted the Queen's press secretary to remind them that although "the princess was a much-loved national figure... she was also a mother whose sons miss her deeply. Prince William and Prince Harry themselves want to be with their father and their grandparents at this time in the quiet haven of Balmoral."

The princes returned to London with their father on 5 September, the day before their mother's funeral. Her body was still lying in the chapel at St James's Palace, and they privately went there that evening to view her, the coffin having been specially lowered so that they would be able to see her face for the last time.

The following morning, to the surprise of many, they joined the funeral procession when it moved past St James's Palace and, along with their father, grandfather and uncle, Earl Spencer, proceeded to walk behind the coffin as it slowly made its way to Westminster Abbey.

Debate had privately raged for days about whether the boys should walk in the procession, with William being particularly unwilling to expose his private grief to the crowds that would be gathered for the occasion, but when Prince Philip offered to walk with him he gave in, much later admitting in an interview that he was glad to have done so, although at the time he was bewildered by the public reaction to his mother's death and tried to hide his face behind his hair as he walked. Harry has also since stated that he too is now glad that he took part, having previously struggled with the ordeal, once revealing, "I don't think any child should be asked to do that, under any circumstances."

During the walk, which was often punctuated by the anguished screams and cries of mourners lining the roads, the visibly devastated but dignified boys were kept distracted by their grandfather, Prince Philip, who chatted to them and pointed out the various London landmarks that they were passing.

Later that day they were able to escape the crowds and say a far more private farewell to their mother when her body was finally laid to rest on an island at the Spencer family home in Althorp where she had grown up.

For the public, the death and funeral of Diana, Princess of Wales, marked the terrible and dramatic end of what had been - in more ways than one - a fairy tale. However, for her two grieving boys, William and Harry, it was the beginning of a long and devastating struggle to cope with the crushing loss of an adored parent. How proud she would be of the fine men that they have both become.

SINGLE PARENT

Following the death of Diana, Charles became a single father. Despite his life of privilege, he still faced challenges that will be familiar to any single parent

Words **Catherine Curzon**

When Diana, Princess of Wales, was tragically killed in a car accident in Paris, her young sons, Prince William and Prince Harry, were staying at Balmoral with their father. It was Prince Charles who broke the news to his boys, and from that day forward none of their lives would be the same. Their grief would be scrutinised in the full glare of one of the most intense spotlights any royal family had ever known.

When the two princes were growing up, Diana had always been keen to include them on official tours and tried to give them the closest thing possible to a normal life. As heir to the throne, however, Charles was often occupied with his royal duties and strongly focused on his work and the role he would one day inherit. That's not to say that he wasn't a loving father, but he was a man in constant preparation to assume the eventual role of constitutional monarch, and with Diana happy to involve herself fully in her sons' lives, he was to some extent publicly regarded as a figure who existed on the sidelines of family life.

With Diana's death, Charles's role in the lives of the two young princes was forced to change overnight. In the face of a blinding media spotlight he did his best to balance the expectations of the nation with his own grief and the need to support William and Harry. Some decisions brought down the wrath of the public on his head, especially when the boys walked behind their mother's funeral procession, but despite his critics, Charles was determined that he wouldn't let his sons down. What he didn't do, of course, was become a full-time, ever-present parent. The boys continued to attend boarding school and Charles continued with his royal duties, but he did so in the knowledge that he was now the sole parent, and he would surely have been aware that of the two parents the boys had once had, he had always been the more distant.

In fact, Charles was the father his own upbringing had made him. The Duke of Edinburgh and Charles had a famously strained relationship, with the timid young Charles sent to his father's old schools despite being woefully unsuited to the harsh regimes at the institutions where he was to study. Prince Philip had been a sporty and confident youth while Charles was anything but, and he was mercilessly bullied as a result of his perceived shortcomings. The Duke of Edinburgh, who barely knew his own father, spoke openly on the differences between himself and his eldest son and acknowledged that their outlooks on the world were poles apart. Nobody knew that more keenly than his eldest son. During his unforgiving school years Charles was forced to develop a protective carapace, and it has remained resolutely difficult to crack throughout Charles's adult years.

The death of Diana, however, left him with no choice. He was perhaps the most high-profile single father on the planet and he was determined that his sons would be allowed the time and space to

Charles's former assistant Tiggy Legge-Bourke was a much-needed female influence for William and Harry following Diana's death

CAMILLA, WILLIAM AND HARRY

Once vilified by the press and painted as a wicked stepmother, Camilla is now very much a part of her stepson's lives

Camilla's relationship with the princes has become stronger over the years

Camilla Parker Bowles was once the other woman, painted as a homewrecker and distrusted by a public who had rallied behind Diana, Princess of Wales, as the royal marriage fell apart. In reality the truth was very different, and since their wedding in 2005 Charles and Camilla have been the model of a happy couple. The Duchess of Cornwall has won the approval of the public, while at home she has proven to be a sensitive and caring stepmother.

Charles put his personal life on hold in the wake of Diana's death and focused instead on his sons, but over the years he and Camilla resumed their romance. When they became an official couple, all people wanted to know was how she was getting on with the young princes. The answer was very well. Prince Harry dismissed any suggestion she was a wicked stepmother and said that far from feeling sorry for him and William, they should instead feel sympathy for the Duchess, who has endured intense scrutiny thanks to her long relationship with Charles. It was a mark of the young prince's newfound maturity that his father and stepmother must have been grateful to hear.

grieve away from the media glare. When Charles went overseas following the death of the princess he often took the boys with him, deepening a relationship that he had already been at pains to improve when he and Diana divorced. He became a familiar figure at the boys' school plays just as his late ex-wife had been, sending notes of appreciation to his sons after each performance. It was a world away from when Prince Philip had attended Charles's own turn in the title role of Shakespeare's *Macbeth*. The young man was mortified when his father laughed his way through the production, mocking Charles's performance from the audience.

Charles, who has always been devoted to duty, made conscious changes to his lifestyle with the intention of helping his sons. He and the Queen did everything possible to maintain their privacy as they grew up and Charles established a rule that he would always be at home whenever Prince William was, regardless of whatever occasion may arise to call him away. Mindful that his company alone wasn't sufficient balm for the bereaved princes, he brought his former assistant, Tiggy Legge-Bourke, back into the family's inner circle. She, along with the Queen, provided a much-needed female influence for William and Harry. Legge-Bourke had previously been a companion to the boys during the infamous War of the Waleses, when Diana had suspected her and Charles of having an affair. After Diana publicly accused her of aborting the Prince of Wales's baby and insisted that she spend as little time with William and Harry as possible, Legge-Bourke had even begun legal proceedings against the princess, though these were subsequently dropped.

Perhaps mindful of his late wife's opinion of Tiggy Legge-Bourke, Charles was at pains to ensure that Diana's family were equally present in the life of his sons. He actively encouraged Diana's sisters, Baroness Jane Fellowes and Lady Sarah McCorquodale, to be a part of their nephews' lives and to provide a link to the late princess that he perhaps couldn't. Showing a sensitivity that he's often been accused of lacking, however, the one person whom Charles didn't bring into their lives for a long time was Camilla Parker Bowles, a former girlfriend with whom he had later conducted an extramarital affair.

Yet as the princes grew, the public and tabloid fascination with their late mother never dimmed and for Harry in particular the grieving process proved to be a struggle. When rumours of his excessive drinking and experimenting with cannabis appeared in the press, Prince Charles acted swiftly and decisively, far from the distant and disinterested figure of lore. Rather than deny the rumours, Charles, who has acted as a patron for numerous drug charities, took the news calmly. He didn't remonstrate with his youngest son but instead acknowledged that such experimentation was all part of growing up in the modern era and was better met with education than punishment. Charles arranged for his youngest to spend a day at a rehabilitation clinic in London, where Harry met recovering addicts and learned about the damage that seemingly harmless experimentation could do.

The approach, typical of Charles's reasoned and balanced approach to parenting, worked. Harry was shocked at what he learned during his day in the

Prince Charles and his two sons spend some quality time together at Sandringham

clinic and scared off any further experimentation. Tales of his excessive drinking dwindled away and he distanced himself from the partying friends who had been photographed raising the roof beside him. Charles also informed the headteacher of Eton College, where Harry was studying, and asked him to keep a watchful eye on the prince, but it was an unnecessary precaution. The short, sharp shock had worked.

Harry, however, wasn't done yet, and he faced an outcry when *The Sun* published photographs of him at a fancy dress party dressed in a Nazi uniform, complete with a swastika armband. Clarence House issued an apology on behalf of the young man, but the public were far from satisfied.

Questions were raised in the media about just how much influence Charles had over his sons and how much discipline they received, while behind the scenes Charles attempted to rein in his son's excesses. As further reports came out of racist language and strip poker in a Las Vegas hotel, it seemed that he hadn't been entirely successful.

Yet to blame Charles for the behaviour of a son, who once confessed that he had always wanted to be a bad boy in his youth, is unfair. In fact, Charles usually attempted to avoid direct confrontation and instead favoured discussion with his sons, recognising that they had grown up in challenging circumstances despite their privilege. Just as the Queen had joined Charles in a concerted effort to keep the boys out of the media spotlight in the aftermath of Diana's death, as they grew older it was she who was often called upon to provide discipline. Charles remained the peacemaker, carefully carving out his relationship with the grieving princes.

On one occasion, however, Charles did admit to having strong words with William after the young man told zoologist Dr Jane Goodall that he was ashamed of the amount of ivory that was in the Buckingham Palace collection. If it were up to him, said William, he'd destroy the lot. This time Charles didn't hold his tongue despite his revulsion for the market in modern ivory and the

Charles has done all that he can to prepare William to one day rule as king

poachers who fuel it. Mindful of his duty to protect the royal brand and passionate about the history of the artefacts under discussion, he told William that his comments had been naïve and ill-informed. For Charles, who spent decades preparing to reign, some things were better left unsaid.

Despite the highly publicised reports of his relationship with Camilla Parker Bowles, Prince Charles purposefully put his personal life on hold in the years following Diana's death. At a time of immense grief and upheaval for his sons, his first priority was to them. However, as time passed and Charles looked to return to some semblance of normality, he made the boys aware that Camilla was going to remain an important part of his life going forward. According to some sources, William and Harry refused to meet Camilla at first, though this has never been confirmed by any member of the royal family. Today, the princes and their stepmother enjoy a warm relationship.

As William and Harry got older, their career paths took them into the military and onto lives of their own. By now happily remarried to Camilla, Charles has remained a watchful and guiding presence, if still exhibiting some of the perceived distance that has been so often commented on by numerous spectators.

Naturally, the press and royal watchers alike remain constantly alert to any suggestion that things aren't rosy in the royal family, and when Prince William married Kate Middleton and the couple welcomed their first child, Prince George, rumours began to spread that Charles's nose had been pushed rather out of joint.

When newspapers claimed that Charles had bitterly complained that the new parents wouldn't let him spend any quality time with his grandson, the feeding frenzy began again. Once again the press reminded the public that Charles and his sons had never been the most demonstrative of families, and now, they claimed, that disharmony was rearing up again.

Though the Palace rushed to dismiss the reports of friction at the heart of the royal family as fanciful, the stories didn't stop and instead the media dug up rumours that the couple were closer to the Middletons than they were to Charles and Duchess of Cornwall and that William preferred to spend more time with his in-laws than he ever did with his own father.

However, while it's true that the couple have made more frequent visits to the Middleton household than to Highgrove, William has sung the effusive praises of Charles as a grandfather and both Charles and Camilla have spoken publicly about their deep love for their grandchildren, on both sides of the family. Quibbles around access and sharing time with grandchildren is something that is likely familiar to many grandparents from all walks of life, so perhaps we should take these rumours with a large dose of salt.

The most intriguing tales of Charles's life as a single father, however, are reserved for Prince Harry. There were rumours that Harry resented his father for favouring William, who was heir to the throne, particularly given the decision Charles had made to always be at home for William's school holidays, while he made no such distinction for Harry. Critics and pundits pointed out the differences between William and Charles too, keen to flag up how much the princes' characters resembled their hands-on, caring mother rather than their apparently distant father. Despite his own misdemeanours, however, Harry's relationship with Charles – at least temporarily – turned the corner when he married former actress Meghan Markle in May 2018. The Duchess of Sussex acted as a peacemaker between the two, helping father and son to overcome their differences. It's certainly no coincidence that when Meghan's own father couldn't walk her down the aisle, it was Charles who proudly took his place.

However, relations between the couple and the rest of the royal family have since become increasingly strained in the wake of the Sussexes' departure from the royal fold and an explosive interview with US talk show host Oprah Winfrey while the late Prince Philip was seriously ill.

The life of a single parent is never an easy one, no matter how privileged and wealthy the family concerned. Charles's own upbringing had been challenging, and when he was left alone to raise his sons in the full and unforgiving blaze of the limelight he was thrust into a role which was more public than ever before. Yet, despite challenges both public and personal, Charles ultimately prevailed.

Single parent

Charles has tried to be a guide and mentor to his sons, sometimes against the odds

FATHER OF THE GROOMS

Regardless of whatever friction may have existed behind the scenes, Charles put on a show for the weddings of his sons

When Prince William announced his engagement to Kate Middleton, it reawakened interest in the Prince's supposedly sometimes strained relationship with his father, Charles. Charles, however, would never have dreamed of being anything but deeply involved in the weddings of his children. Though they had lost their mother, their father was determined to be there for them on this most important of days.

Charles wasn't William's best man – that honour went to Harry – but he was beaming in pride of place at Westminster Abbey. The lamb served at the wedding supper came from Charles's farm and the newlyweds left their Buckingham Palace reception in Charles's Aston Martin, which the Queen had given him as a gift for his 21st birthday.

When it came to the wedding of Harry and Meghan, Charles served in one of the most important roles there was. The bride's father, Thomas, was prevented from walking her down the aisle by ill health and instead she asked a delighted Charles to do the honours. Sadly, the image of a smiling Charles and Meghan on the wedding day is one that has not endured despite it symbolising the acceptance of a new generation of royals by the old.

Charles and Camilla arrive together at a church in Mey, Scotland, to attend a service in 2002

REKINDLING TRUE LOVE

It was an affair that rocked the world and sparked a considerable amount of in-fighting, but Charles would ultimately get his happily ever after

Words **Katherine Marsh**

They called it 'Camillagate'. Charles's marriage to Diana was already shaky at best, but what was unveiled was explosive, and it spelled the end for one of the world's most celebrated couples. Recorded in the late 1980s, the tapes were recordings of a clandestine phone call between Charles and the married Camilla Parker Bowles, his first love, and they left nothing to the imagination. Charles and Camilla were having an affair, and now the whole world knew.

As it turns out, the couple had never lost contact. After they had both married they remained in regular correspondence - Charles apparently even phoned Camilla while he was on his honeymoon. Stephen Barry, Charles's valet, perhaps summed it up best: "Camilla was a habit he could not break, an obsession he did not wish to conquer." It's a highly accurate statement, and especially so after the start of the affair.

According to Charles himself, for most of the 1980s their relationship was purely amicable, but that all changed in 1986. His marriage was falling apart around him, Diana becoming more distant, so he retreated to comfort - and that comfort was in the arms of his first love. They grew closer and closer, with Charles beginning to plan visits for when Camilla's husband, Andrew, and their children were away. On other occasions, one of Charles's retainers would make the 15-minute drive to Middlewick House to deliver notes, packages and flowers that Charles had picked himself. He was besotted with his 'other woman', but their clandestine affair would prove his undoing.

However much he tried to hide his mistress, Camilla's presence hung over Charles's marriage. The two were almost constantly in contact, and it was becoming harder to hide. In autumn 1998, rumours of royal infidelity were beginning to circulate, and *Vanity Fair* went so far as to report that Charles was "relaxing with the sympathetic wives of older friends". Then it all came crumbling down: Diana found out.

In 1989, Diana mustered up the courage to approach her husband's paramour. "I would just like you to know that I know exactly what is going on between you and Charles - I wasn't born yesterday," she told Camilla. "I'm sorry I'm in the way, I obviously am in the way, and it must be hell for both of you, but I do know what is going on. Don't treat me like an idiot." Diana often referred to Camilla as 'the Rottweiler' - she was well aware that Camilla was a threat.

What made it worse was that Diana found out just how many people had been helping Charles cover up his affair. The list included people who Diana had taken into her confidence, and she was absolutely heartbroken at the revelation.

Charles and Diana separated in 1992, and just over a year later a bombshell interview was aired as Charles found himself in the firing line of Jonathan Dimbleby. Matters came to a head when he admitted that he had been faithful to his wife "until it became irretrievably broken down, us both having tried". While he only referred to Camilla as "a great friend", the damage had irrevocably been done as newspaper headlines boldly declared "Charles: I cheated on Diana" and "Di told you so". Camilla's relatively quiet life was turned upside down, and some outraged women even threw bread rolls at her in a supermarket.

A year later, Camilla and Andrew Parker Bowles were divorced, and the Waleses followed soon afterwards in 1996. Camilla was still around, though. Charles hosted a 50th birthday party for her in July 1997 at Highgrove House, a way of slowly bringing her into the royal fold and introducing her to the British public, but the people didn't warm to the idea. In the same month, a TV poll showed that almost half of participants thought that if Camilla and Charles married, the then heir should be disqualified from kingship. Diana was the much-loved princess of the people, not Camilla - but the former was about to become the People's Princess.

In August 1997, tragedy struck. Fleeing from the paparazzi in Paris, the car Diana was travelling in crashed and she lost her life as a result of her extensive internal injuries. The outpouring

Camilla sits a row behind her partner at a concert to celebrate the Queen's Golden Jubilee in June 2002

Opposition to Charles's relationship with Camilla was rife as a result of Diana's popularity

"PEAT WAS UNDER ORDERS FROM THE QUEEN TO BREAK UP CHARLES AND CAMILLA. THE PLAN BACKFIRED"

of grief from around the world was phenomenal – over 1 million bouquets were left outside the gates of Kensington Palace – and attitudes towards Camilla soured even more. As a result, she disappeared from the public sphere, but she never really went away.

At events, Charles and Camilla would arrive and leave separately, and a charity function that had been due to take place in September 1997 was cancelled as the pair were apparently scheduled to appear together.

But the couple didn't separate. In 1998 Camilla met Prince William for the first time at St James's Palace. It wasn't planned – Camilla had become a regular visitor there and William dropped by unexpectedly – but the meeting went well, with the two later having tea twice as well as being seen together at a shared lunch. She met Prince Harry soon after. In fact, in 1999 the four were seen on holiday together in Greece.

Yet even though Charles and Camilla were very much in love with each other, the Queen was livid. She strongly disapproved of their relationship, allegedly referring to her son's paramour as "that wicked woman". That didn't stop Charles, and in 1999 he appeared in public with Camilla for the first time at a birthday party for Camilla's sister at the Ritz in London. It was becoming clearer that Charles wouldn't leave her.

A year later, the Queen's animosity seemed to be starting to fade. She accepted an invitation to an event at Highgrove, knowing full well that Camilla would be there, and it formed part of a plan that would show Camilla was non-negotiable to Charles. The initiative saw their first public kiss in 2001 at an event for the National Osteoporosis Society, and more was to come.

In 2002, Charles found a new private secretary in Sir Michael Peat, but there was a catch – Peat was under instruction from the Queen to break up Charles and Camilla. The plan backfired. It didn't take long for Peat to realise that the couple would never part, and as a result he became one of their fiercest advocates. In doing so, he told Charles that he needed to marry his love or she had to go, and this idea was backed up by Camilla's father,

Rekindling true love

Charles and Camilla leave the Queen's Theatre in London after a performance in January 2000

Bruce Shand, who said, "I want to meet my maker knowing my daughter's all right."

Peat had come from Buckingham Palace, and his close connections with the staff there came in handy. He had a word with Sir Robin Janvrin, the Queen's private secretary, who was also on Charles's side, and he in turn advised the Queen. Then an all-out media offensive got underway.

The tabloids had been having great fun with their royal stories over the years, painting Camilla as an evil homewrecker who had ruined the lives of Diana, William and Harry. The scandal sold incredibly well, but Kensington Palace started a major campaign to change Camilla's image, pushing her reputation as a charitable and kind woman with a keen love of gardening and the outdoors. The main aim was to humanise her but not make her too popular - that rivalry between Charles and Diana had been too explosive to repeat. Colleen Harris, one of Charles's former press secretaries, claimed, "The more we made Camilla acceptable, the less the [outrageous stories] had traction." It was working.

Finally, in 2003, it was announced that Charles was to move into Clarence House, the home of Queen Elizabeth The Queen Mother until her death the year prior. But that wasn't the only information that the announcement contained - it turned out that Camilla had been helping with the refurbishment of the building and she was to have a private office to accommodate her personal assistants. However, it was stressed that Camilla would "continue to maintain" her own house in Wiltshire, and no formal suite would be hers. Instead, she would share with Charles.

Camilla was becoming the permanent fixture that Charles had always wanted her to be. She was a part of his diary meetings, helped focus his mind and ensured his attendance at events. Rumours began to swell about a possible royal engagement, and opposition to the idea was beginning to wane as the nation healed from the death of Diana. They wouldn't have too long to wait - having had to be apart for so long in the 1980s, Charles wasn't about to let Camilla slip away again.

MRS PARKER BOWLES
The story of Camilla and Andrew's marriage

Theirs was an odd relationship. From the get-go, Andrew had never been entirely faithful to Camilla, and that didn't stop after their wedding day on 4 July 1973. While Camilla fell into her affair with Charles, Andrew had started up a long-term relationship with Rosemary Pitman.

Nonetheless, their marriage was relatively happy, and Camilla and Andrew had two children together. Tom was born just over a year after the wedding, on 18 December 1974, while a girl, Laura, arrived on 1 January 1978. Both children were brought up as Catholics, like their father, but Camilla never steered away from Anglicanism. Even in these early days of their marriage, Charles was never far away - in fact he was made Tom's godfather.

Despite infidelities on the part of both Camilla and Andrew - they were both aware of the other's - after Charles's explosive interview in which he admitted his affair to the world, Andrew changed his tune. The couple divorced in 1995, but they didn't give a specific reason, instead calling it a "private matter" and saying that they had "rather different interests". Just a year later Andrew was married to Rosemary and Camilla was becoming closer to Charles.

Camilla and Andrew on their wedding day in 1973

A relaxed Charles and Camilla greet well-wishers after the second part of their wedding festivities

Charles was part of the largest gathering of world leaders ever at the funeral of John Paul II

KEEPING THE GROOM WAITING

After 34 years, a last-minute hitch led to further delay

An unexpected delay to the royal wedding was announced on 4 April, just four days before Charles and Camilla were due to wed – the ceremony would be postponed for 24 hours, to Saturday 9 April. The reason was the death of Pope John Paul II, who breathed his last on 2 April; Charles was despatched to the Vatican as the Queen's representative at the Pope's funeral on the day that he should have been tying the knot. After the funerary rites were complete, Charles flew home and spent the night before his wedding with William and Harry at Highgrove House.

The death of the Pope also threw the souvenir industry into a panic. The Royal Mint hastily recalled their commemorative coins, while Royal Mail decided to plough ahead despite their commemorative stamp packs having the wrong date. The china and ceramics that traditionally marked these occasions had to be dumped or re-stamped, although some clever buyers deliberately snapped up souvenirs with the wrong date on in the hope that they would be more collectable than the correct ones. However, it could have been much worse – Charles's second marriage only had around 25 official products, whereas his first had 1,600.

The official photos captured genuine smiles on the faces of both families

After an initially lukewarm reception from the British people and press, Camilla was gradually accepted as a potential royal spouse

THE WEDDING OF CHARLES AND CAMILLA

Charles's second marriage was a unique take on the royal wedding

Words Scott Reeves

On Saturday 9 April 2005, Charles and Camilla Parker Bowles were finally married 34 years after they first met, although just two months after their engagement was announced. The details as to how Charles popped the question were kept private, but the public and press had enough to discuss without learning whether Charles went down on bended knee. Although the Church of England allowed the marriage of divorcees whose spouses were still living – as was the case for Camilla – some were uncomfortable with the idea of the future supreme governor of the Church of England marrying a divorcee in a religious ceremony.

Constitutional experts were dragged from their ivory towers to perform for the press and consider the legality of the forthcoming nuptials. Several members of the public wrote objections to the Cirencester and Chippenham register offices, although all were rejected. Some suggested a compromise by marrying in the Church of Scotland, as Princess Anne did when she married Timothy Laurence after having divorced Mark Phillips, but that idea was dismissed.

Instead, Charles and Camilla opted to have a royal wedding unlike any before: a civil ceremony at a licensed non-religious venue followed by a special service of blessing at St George's Chapel at Windsor Castle. Rowan Williams, the Archbishop of Canterbury, made clear his support for their choices when he said, "These arrangements have my strong support and are consistent with Church of England guidelines concerning remarriage, which the Prince of Wales fully accepts as a committed Anglican and as prospective supreme governor of the Church of England."

The couple's first choice of venue for the civil marriage, Windsor Castle, was soon found to be unsuitable. If the castle was granted a licence to hold civil weddings it would have to be made available for other couples to use for three years. Instead, Charles and Camilla moved the civil ceremony to Windsor Guildhall, just outside the castle walls.

It may have been a unique royal wedding, but tradition still played a role. Camilla's engagement ring was a Windsor family heirloom that had belonged to Queen Elizabeth The Queen Mother, while the wedding rings were made from 22 carat Welsh gold from the Clogau St David's mine in Bontddu, as most royal wedding rings had been since the marriage of Prince Albert and Elizabeth Bowes-Lyon in 1923.

On the morning of the wedding, a nervous-looking Camilla stepped out of the car carrying her and Charles, perhaps having heard a few boos on the streets of Windsor. However, the majority of the crowd soon found their voice and were clearly there to cheer the bride, who was wearing a cream silk chiffon dress and matching coat from Robinson Valentine with a wide-brimmed hat by Philip Treacy.

Only 28 people were invited to the intimate civil ceremony, all of whom were members of the bride or groom's families. Prince William and Tom Parker Bowles served as the witnesses, although the Queen and Duke of Edinburgh were noticeable by their absence. The official reason why the monarch chose to stay away from the civil ceremony was to keep the occasion low-key, although her discomfort at attending a civil ceremony as head of the Church of England probably played a role in her decision.

The Queen did, however, attend St George's Chapel for what was described as a Service of Prayer and Dedication and hosted the reception afterwards. Camilla changed into a new outfit for the second part of the day, a pale blue dress hand-embroidered with gold thread with a gold-leaf feather and Swarovski diamond headdress. In front of 800 guests and television cameras, Charles and Camilla knelt before the Archbishop of Canterbury and read what was described as "the strongest act of penitence from the 1662 Book of Common Prayer".

Following the ceremony, the newlyweds stepped outside with smiles on their faces. Camilla approached the masses of spectators, thanking them for their good wishes. Any fears that the sinusitis she had been suffering with would spoil the big day were extinguished amid the overwhelmingly positive cheers.

At the reception in the state rooms of Windsor Castle, Charles toasted and thanked his new bride "who has stood with me through thick and thin and whose optimism and humour have seen me through". Although the royal couple were now legally the Prince and Princess of Wales, Camilla chose to style herself the Duchess of Cornwall – using Charles's first subsidiary title – since she was aware that Diana was so strongly associated with the alternative.

The Queen also said a few words and, given the equestrian interest they all shared, chose to compare Charles and Camilla's relationship to the Grand National: "They have overcome Becher's Brook and The Chair and all kinds of other terrible obstacles. They have come through and I'm very proud and wish them well. My son is home and dry with the woman he loves."

LEGACY

102 ## Sport & culture
Being a modern royal means a busy schedule, but King Charles III has always been sure to carve out time to pursue his own interests

106 ## Living in the spotlight
No family on Earth is as scrutinised as the British royal family, and at times King Charles III has clashed with the media

110 ## A family duty
Ever conscious of the opportunities and access his status affords him, King Charles III has worked to bring people together in support of various causes close to his heart

118 ## Dedicated to sustainability
A vocal proponent of green policies and environmental protections long before the current climate crisis, Britain's new king has never been shy when it comes to voicing his opinion on key social matters

124 ## Long live the king
The devastating announcement of Queen Elizabeth II's death in September 2022 plunged a family and a nation into mourning, but as the world paid its respects protocol demanded that a grieving son must prepare to ascend the throne

SPORT AND CULTURE

Though King Charles III takes his royal duties seriously, he still finds time to relax. Though some of his hobbies are well known, just how does he unwind?

Words **Catherine Curzon**

As the heir to the throne for much of his life and the high-profile and well-connected figure behind a number of thriving concerns, Charles III isn't a man who likes to sit back and do nothing. In fact, he has a number of hobbies, from sports to cultural pursuits and even, surprisingly, the arcane arts of magic!

Of course, the most well-known of Charles's hobbies is certainly his ardent love of polo, which he began playing competitively in his youth. In fact, polo has been a family passion for decades, and with Prince Harry and Prince William following in his footsteps as keen players, the Windsor enthusiasm for the game doesn't show any signs of fading yet.

Charles inherited his love of polo from his father Prince Philip, Duke of Edinburgh, who was in turn introduced to the sport by his uncle, Earl Mountbatten of Burma. After his marriage to Elizabeth, Philip made the sport fashionable in London and formed the near-legendary Guards Polo Club, which he was president of from 1955 until his death. It was the Duke of Edinburgh who made a gift of a polo mallet to Charles when he was 15 and bought him his very first polo pony, introducing him to what would become his most ardent sporting interest. Charles began competing professionally after four years of training and devoted hours of time to his passion as he grew older. He played competitively for decades, and even when he retired from competition he continued to play for fun and philanthropy well into his fifties.

Equine pursuits have always been a great favourite of the royal family. Like other members of the House of Windsor, Charles was a keen huntsman, but when he took his sons on a hunt in 1999, the decision was viewed as a political statement - usually a no-no for the royals. In fact, Charles III was so devoted to hunting that he wrote to Prime Minister Tony Blair in an attempt to convince the Labour government not to pursue the ban on blood sports. His efforts failed, and when hunting with hounds was outlawed, Charles had no choice but to abide by the new law. He does, however, continue to shoot and fish and is an advocate of sustainable angling.

Although it's hardly a surprise that Charles enjoys country sports, he might not seem a natural on the football terraces. In 2012, however, he surprised attendees at a Windsor Castle reception when he confessed to being a fan of Burnley FC. Charles explained that he had grown fond of the club thanks to his charity work in the town, and to say thank you the Clarets sent him his very own season ticket, so he need never miss a home match at Turf Moor again.

Yet Charles, of course, is perhaps more associated with pastoral pursuits than the rough and tumble of the grandstand. He has spoken at length of his passion for gardening and particularly the gardens at Highgrove House, which he has cultivated for many years. Charles discovered his love of horticulture as a child when he and Princess Anne were each given a little plot of their own in the grounds of Buckingham Palace. He spent every moment he could caring for his plot and soon expanded beyond its limits, taking on more and more responsibility and studying the subject as he grew. As a result, the king has become an acknowledged expert on horticulture and has turned his hobby into action, speaking to the media and various flagship outlets such as *Gardeners' World* about his fears for the ecological future of the British landscape. Having personally planted many of the hedges on Duchy Home Farm, he has even hosted the National Hedgelaying Championships there.

Charles has happily spoken to the press about the relaxation he gains from working in his garden and also about his penchant for talking to the trees and plants that he has cultivated. Though some commentators questioned whether this might cast doubt over Charles's faculties, he insisted he still had all his marbles.

Charles inherited his love of polo from his father Prince Philip

Instead Charles turned his unusual pastime to the advantage of the environment again, using interest in his admission to discuss the importance of understanding and respecting the landscape, as well as helping it flourish in any way possible. For Charles, if talking to the trees might be to the benefit of the natural landscape, then it is a conversation he is more than happy to have.

Although the king is inarguably a man of the land, he is also a lover of cultural pursuits and has indulged in more than a few of them himself. Charles is a keen watercolourist who has exhibited his work professionally, and he's also an author, having written and published books in a variety of genres. One of these was *The Old Man of Lochnagar*, which began life as a story a young Charles made up to entertain his little brothers. From its humble origins, *The Old Man of Lochnagar* went on to a life of its own as a stage musical and ballet, as well as a short film narrated by Charles. In fact, Charles even went on to read the story to children all over the country during an episode of *Jackanory*.

Perhaps it's only natural that *The Old Man of Lochnagar* flourished on stage, because Charles has long been a patron of the arts and has championed many organisations across the country. A keen student of music in his youth, Charles revived the position of official harpist to the court and is a regular visitor to theatres and concert venues. Though he's the president of the Royal Shakespeare Company, Charles's artistic preferences aren't always for what might be considered the highbrow either, and for a time during his years as a student he even considered following his comedy idols into the spotlight.

The king is famously a fan of *The Goon Show* and when he attended Cambridge University he joined the Footlights and began to develop his own cast of absurd comedy characters. Legend has it that he needs little prompting to launch into an impromptu rendition of the infamous *Ying Tong Song*, and he even committed his love of the Goons to film, recording himself impersonating

Sport and culture

Charles's love of skiing is one that he shares with his family

Charles has been a keen horticulturalist since his youth and is passionate about sharing his hobby with a new generation of gardeners

During his polo career Charles raised a staggering £12 million for charity

POLO ACCIDENTS

Though Charles is passionate about polo, injuries eventually forced him to retire from the sport he loves

After decades of playing polo and more than his fair share of broken bones, in 2005 Charles finally announced that he was going to retire from the hobby that he described as "my one great extravagance".

In 1980, Charles was thrown from his horse and kicked, leaving him with a facial scar. Like any sportsperson he accepted the risk of injury as part of the game, but in 1990 he suffered his first really serious injury when he suffered a severe fracture of his arm after a fall. His recovery was complicated and for a time there was even a risk that he could lose the use of his limb permanently.

As the press and public began to ask whether the heir to the throne should be taking such risks, Charles doubled down. He loved polo and used it as an escape from domestic troubles. However, back problems led Charles to rethink his decision, and the final straw for his polo career came in 2001 when a serious fall in front of his sons left him unconscious and in need or urgent medical attention.

Peter Sellers in character as Bluebottle, famed for his bizarre, high-pitched tones. Perhaps inevitably, Charles eventually befriended Goon Spike Milligan, and the two spent long and happy hours together, dining and cementing their friendship.

Of course, those who didn't know how close Charles and the Goon had become were stunned when Milligan called him a "grovelling little bastard" on live TV. Charles found the incident hilarious and though Milligan later sent a tongue-in-cheek apology and asked whether a knighthood was out of the question, it wasn't. Spike Milligan duly received his knighthood.

For a man who is often thought of as being rather serious, there is one last interest that may surprise people. In 1975, Charles auditioned for membership of the illustrious Magic Circle by performing the famous cup and balls illusion. He was successful and was welcomed into the secretive circle.

Today the king has shown no signs of slowing down. He continues to write and paint and spends many hours working in the gardens that he adores. He hasn't lost his taste for the spotlight either, and in 2016 he achieved a lifelong ambition and appeared at the Royal Shakespeare Theatre to join the celebrations for Shakespeare Live. In the midst of a comical debate about the delivery of *Hamlet*'s most infamous line, Charles strode onto the stage and showed everyone just how it was done.

LIVING IN THE SPOTLIGHT

From his turbulent youth to life as the widower of Wales and beyond, Charles III has never really had the easiest relationship with the press

Words Catherine Curzon

Charles has long since become an old and practised hand at dealing with the press. Whether trying his first taste of alcohol, weathering the storm of his marriage breakdown or negotiating the choppy waters of widowhood and life as a single parent, his relationship with the media is one that has had more than its fair share of ups and downs.

As a little boy, Charles followed his father as a pupil at Cheam Boarding School in Hampshire. It was one of the most gruelling and miserable periods in the life of the young prince, and he was bullied mercilessly by his peers. Yet it was during his years at Cheam that Charles realised that the media would always be an integral part of his life. While sitting in the headmaster's study watching his mother Elizabeth II perform the closing ceremony of the Commonwealth Games in Cardiff, the nine-year-old Charles was stunned to hear her announce that he would henceforth be given the title of Prince of Wales. It was the moment he realised just how very different he was from the boys who tormented him.

As a shy and rather lonely little boy, Charles could always count on the friendship of his protection officer, Donald Green. Green was something of a mentor to the isolated prince, a constant and supportive figure in a world that was sorely lacking in them. His eventual fate was also a salutary lesson to the young Prince of Wales on the power of the press.

When Charles was just 15 and a pupil at Gordonstoun, his father's other alma mater, he and four other pupils were given permission to sail the school ketch, the Pinta, to Stornoway on the Isle of Lewis. Upon reaching the island the boys made for the local hotel while Green headed for the cinema to purchase tickets for his charges. With the locals gathering to stare at him, Charles fled to the quieter back rooms of the hotel, where he found himself in a bar. He ordered and was served a cherry brandy, which he'd drunk before during shooting trips. Though it's hardly the first time an underage schoolboy has drunk alcohol, most underage schoolboys aren't heirs to the throne, and as luck would have it, there happened to be a tabloid reporter in the bar too. The next day the story of that afternoon brandy was splashed across the headlines. Though it may seem absurd, only the Profumo affair was bigger news.

As a result of the scandal Green was dismissed and Charles lost one of his most precious friends. It's hardly surprising that in years to come, his relationship with the media was one of distrust.

As Charles grew older and speculation mounted about his bachelor status, the press fell over itself to report every twist and turn in his personal life. For a reserved young man like the then Prince of Wales, the intrusion was immense and reached its peak in 1977 when the *Daily Express* wrongly reported that he was about to announce his engagement to Princess Marie Astrid of Luxembourg. In fact there was to be no such betrothal. Charles, famously, was to marry someone else entirely.

When he announced his engagement to Lady Diana Spencer it marked the beginning of one of the most troubled eras of his life. The couple navigated the merry-go-round of press calls and photo sessions together, but from the off the shy bride-to-be captivated the nation and the media alike. The bride and groom were photographed for *Vogue* following an exclusive interview for the BBC, and a staggering 750 million viewers tuned in to watch the wedding of the century in July 1981.

Once Charles and Diana were married, the royal couple were subject to a media spotlight like neither of them had ever seen before. Speculation about the state of the royal marriage reached fever pitch with the publication of Andrew Morton's explosive book, *Diana: Her True Story*, which lifted the lid on alleged affairs between Charles and his former girlfriend Camilla Parker Bowles, as well as Diana's relationship with her former riding instructor, Major James Hewitt.

During a family trip to the ski resort of Klosters, Charles was caught on tape giving his frank opinion on the press

Although the latter affair didn't begin until two years after the birth of Prince Harry, the press took one look at the redheaded Hewitt and the redheaded little boy and began to drop hints about the 'real' parentage of the young prince.

The newspapers were filled with salacious details of the love lives of the then Prince and Princess of Wales, and seemingly not a day passed when they weren't making the headlines. From tales of extramarital affairs to damning transcripts of explicit conversations between Charles and Camilla Parker Bowles, the world followed the twists and turns of the breakdown of the royal marriage with unconcealed enthusiasm. It came as no surprise to anybody when the separation of Charles and Diana was officially announced, and as the press and public took sides, Charles found himself cast as the definite villain of the piece.

Although he had always attempted to maintain his privacy, Charles fought back and agreed to an interview with Jonathan Dimbleby, but viewing figures and audience response paled beside Diana's interview with *Panorama* the following year. Never before had the press been so deeply entrenched in the lives of such senior royals. From that day until her death two years later, Diana was rarely out of the media spotlight.

Over the years of his estrangement from Diana, Charles felt the intrusion of the press like never before, and it led to a deep distrust. His most intimate business was front-page news and he was pilloried time and again for the breakdown of his marriage while garnering little sympathy. It was hardly surprising that his loathing of the media deepened still further, a fact that was made embarrassingly public in 2005 during a photocall with his sons ahead of his wedding to Camilla Parker Bowles. As the press prepared for the traditional media appearance, Charles's microphone picked up his whispers about how much he loathed press calls with these "bloody people", particularly the BBC's royal pundit, Nicholas Witchell.

Although apologies were later made, it was the beginning of his fightback against the media. His press team was revealed to exercise editorial rights over any interviews with Charles, while in the face of his happy second marriage and increasing protests over press intrusion, the vitriolic reports on his private life have largely faded away. While his ascension to the throne thrust him back into the spotlight, prior to him becoming king the press had turned its attentions to his sons and their marriages. Instead he has become an elder statesman, successfully transforming public opinion of himself. He will no doubt continue to pursue his personal passions as king, but his approach to exploring his interests and supporting the causes close to his heart may well change due to the expectations placed upon a ruling sovereign.

However, he is very much his own man, one forged in the crucible of decades of acute public scrutiny. Few people have faced the anger and intrusion of the media with quite the force that Charles has. Fewer still have emerged from the story to give interviews to the likes of Ant and Dec alongside the very wife who it once seemed would never be accepted. Charles and Camilla, however, have navigated the stormy waters of the tabloids on their own terms and survived. As king and queen consort, they will continue to flourish.

Living in the spotlight

The interest in the engagement of Charles and Diana exacerbated a troublesome relationship with the press

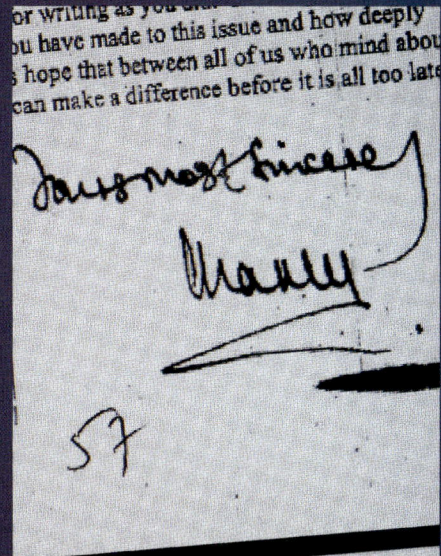

Charles's black spider memos took their name from his distinctive signature

THE BLACK SPIDER MEMOS

When Charles's memos to senior politicians were published by the *Guardian* the outcome was surprising

The so-called 'black spider' memos were a series of communications sent by Charles to senior government figures while he was still Prince of Wales. Their nickname came about as a result of his very distinctive 'spidery' handwriting.

Traditionally, the British monarch and their heirs have been politically neutral, but the memos seemed to suggest that Charles might have been attempting to meddle and use his influence to direct government policy. When journalist Rob Evans made a Freedom of Information request for the letters in 2010, it began a chain of legal hearings that eventually found in favour of the release. The papers were published in the *Guardian* in 2015 and largely concerned Charles's interest in subjects such as the environment, architecture and social welfare, none of which came as a surprise.

Although the media attempted to interpret Charles's correspondence as proof of his inappropriate involvement in political matters, the public were underwhelmed. Instead the reaction was mostly positive, with people pleased to see that the concerns of a senior royal reflected their own. There was little if any evidence that Charles had attempted to influence government policy and he emerged from the black spider memos non-story with his reputation intact.

A FAMILY DUTY

As Prince of Wales, Charles was the heir to the British throne, in itself is a full-time job. As a senior royal, he had no shortage of duties and had to develop a work ethic to match, an approach that will now serve him well as king

Words **Catherine Curzon**

It's not always easy to be the heir to the throne. In a near-perpetual existence as the man not of today, but tomorrow, the men who have previously carried the title of Princes of Wales have struggled to find a role or a place in the world beyond king-in-waiting, slipping into scandal and dissolution as a result. For Charles, however, that wasn't a problem. Like his mother, the late Queen Elizabeth II, Charles has always prided himself on his unshakeable work ethic and his dedication to duty and country. Far from waiting to inherit the crown from his once seemingly indefatigable mother, he carved out a place for himself as a businessman, charity patron and prince who took his duties seriously.

Charles was invested as Prince of Wales by his mother in July 1969, when she felt that the young man was becoming ready to take on a more senior role in the royal family. As a title with a rich history that carried the weight of many expectations, Charles understood the responsibility that he had been given and was determined to make the most of it, using it not for personal advancement but to represent the royal family across the world. Contrary to popular belief, there is no official constitutional role for the heir to the throne, and this in itself caused plenty of problems in the past. Charles, however, perhaps did more than any other Prince of Wales in generations to develop his own role and build it over the decades as he edged ever closer towards becoming king. While being crowned monarch would come with its own inevitable sadness and loss, Charles was always acutely aware of his eventual fate and was determined to be ready to step directly into the rank of king, thus ensuring no period of instability for the country at a seminal moment in its history.

Charles has always aimed to unite people regardless of background or role and create a nation that is unified and celebrates its own achievements and those of its citizens. Leading by example, as the Prince of Wales he highlighted the importance of charitable and community engagement, visiting organisations ranging from vast multinationals to local endeavours and bringing with him the gratitude and good wishes of the royal family.

Throughout her reign, Elizabeth II remained a thoroughly engaged and active monarch, with a packed official diary. However, there were naturally times when Elizabeth II wasn't able to accept every engagement that came her way, and one of Charles's main roles, in fact one that expanded as the years passed, was supporting his mother as she carried out her duties. Alongside his wife Camilla (now the queen consort), Charles represented his mother as the national figurehead both at home and across the globe, and he has proven to be an extremely skilful spokesperson.

In his supporting role to Elizabeth II, Charles was often found hosting visiting dignitaries on state visits. Like all of the family he is an ambassador for the United Kingdom, and particularly as his mother grew older, Charles stepped into her shoes to attend state occasions overseas. These included official tours or even state funerals. On these trips abroad Charles was a valuable non-partisan figure who was able to draw awareness to overseas concerns as well as oversees charitable initiatives in the Commonwealth and further afield. As a politically neutral ambassador, his loyalty was to the crown. He does, however, hold a number of personal special interests including the armed forces, in which he has served, and fostering special relationships with countries overseas both inside and outside of the Commonwealth.

"Charles has always aimed to unite people"

Charles's presence brought a welcome injection of media interest for community initiatives he supported

THE PRINCE'S TRUST

Charles has long since been a champion of charitable causes. One of the most famous is his own Prince's Trust organisation

The Prince's Trust offers support and skills to young people across the world

Charles established the Prince's Trust in 1976 in order to benefit vulnerable and disadvantaged young people. The charity offers support to 11 to 30 year olds who are struggling at school or unable to find work. It works closely with young people who are about to transition from care into adulthood as well as younger people at risk of exclusion from school. There is also a focus on those who require support with their mental health or may find themselves homeless or facing legal troubles.

The Prince's Trust has established innumerable support and training programmes aimed at giving vulnerable young people all the skills they need to succeed, from building self-confidence to providing financial assistance or practical help with education and employment. The success rate of those who join a Prince's Trust programme is high, and it continues to be one of Charles's greatest personal passions.

The Prince's Trust International has extended the work championed by Charles overseas. It is now the UK's leading youth charity, having carried out projects worth well over a billion pounds. The Prince's Trust has helped almost a million young people reach their personal best, creating entrepreneurs and inspiring a generation to learn, grow and succeed.

As a prince, Charles's most important and passionately pursued duties were his dedication to promoting charitable endeavours both at home and overseas. He was patron of hundreds of charities covering areas from healthcare and overseas development to conservation and his own Prince's Trust, Charles's own charitable organisation. The scope of Charles's charitable interests was reflected in the Prince of Wales's Charities, an official grouping of all the not-for-profit organisations of which the then Prince of Wales served as patron or president. He also presided over the Prince of Wales' Charitable Fund, which was first established in 1979 and exists to incubate fledgling projects and provide grants to fund initiatives that will benefit a large range of causes, with a special focus on education, responsible business, sustainability and the built environment. Throughout his charitable endeavours Charles was no silent partner doling out cash either; he carried out innumerable engagements every year in support of the charities he supported and his involvement proved hugely valuable for them, raising over £100 million annually that could be ploughed back into communities all over the world.

In 2019, Charles's duties as a senior royal were in the headlines a lot. According to press speculation, it was Charles who had taken unenviable responsibility on behalf of the royal family for dealing with the fallout from Prince Andrew's televised interview regarding his friendship with Jeffrey Epstein. It seemed that the then Prince of Wales acted decisively and Prince Andrew speedily withdrew from his official duties to take a step out of the limelight. If this was due to the intervention of Charles as a senior royal, then it provided a revealing glimpse into how he will now likely behave as head of the royal family.

Like his mother before him, Charles is passionate about the countryside, the nation and his privacy. He spent a huge tranche of his life as a man in waiting, and while Elizabeth II never spoke openly about her political views, her son has not been so reserved. Through his lobbying and charitable work he has established himself as a man of strongly held opinions. His name brought with it a leverage that few others could hope to achieve, and he was happy to levy it wherever necessary, including in letters to senior government figures in which he poured out his opinions on environmental and conservation issues.

Even as he has grown older Charles's work ethic hasn't dimmed. When he wasn't tramping the fields of Duchy Home Farm and laying hedges, he was sitting up into the night writing speeches and letters, sometimes working so late that he was found asleep at his desk. Unlike his late mother, Charles is a natural campaigner and this is something that traditionally monarchs shouldn't be. The line between interest and intervention

A family duty

Charles has always been keen to undertake cultural overseas duties

As Prince of Wales and Duchess of Cornwall the royal couple had a packed schedule

is narrow and as head of state his critics will be keenly on the lookout for anything that might suggest he is attempting to meddle in the affairs of the government, no matter how subtly the pressure might be applied.

Throughout much of his life Charles watched his mother reign with her customary quiet dignity. Despite occasional rumours, nobody knew what Elizabeth II's political opinions really were, nor on which side of the fence she sat in the case of the vast majority of topics. Charles, however, is quite the opposite. His opinions and feelings are well-known thanks to his lobbying and occasional - though always eye-opening - interviews, which he retains editorial approval of. One thing we can be sure of is the fact that Charles is incredibly conscientious and will certainly not shirk his responsibilities now as monarch. After all, he has been preparing for the job for decades.

When she took her oath in Westminster Abbey, Queen Elizabeth II accepted that her role as a constitutional monarch meant that she would have no political voice at all. For Charles, of course, there has been no such acceptance. Though there will be points of commonality with his mother, such as a dedicated work ethic and love of the nation, in many other ways Charles will be a very different sort of monarch indeed.

Over the years of waiting Charles was not idle. Instead, he seized the poorly structured role of the Prince of Wales with both hands and moulded it into something that suited his own interests, personality and ambitions. Despite battling with unpopularity and the derision of the press throughout his life, particularly during the breakdown of his first marriage and the aftermath of the death of Diana, Princess of Wales, Charles has clung to the basic belief that he must have a useful role, even if he had to define it himself. He is intelligent, well-read and widely travelled, and he has made the most of his exemplary education to extend his horizons and interests. He has become a champion of charities and a recognised expert on environmental matters, culminating in the 2009 Rainforest Summit at St James's Palace, in which he presided over a meeting of senior international policymakers, all of them gathered together to discuss climate change. This gathering of experts and influential politicians was unlike anything the royal family had ever seen and it was certainly unlike anything that Elizabeth II would have personally involved herself in. As the new head of state it's unlikely that Charles will now completely forgo his interests or fall silent on his concerns.

Charles is unique in the monarchy: he is the first British monarch to have attended boarding school as opposed to having been educated at home. Though he may not seem like the model of modern monarchy, Charles is unlike any sovereign the country has known before. He grew up in one of the most changeable periods in British history and certainly one of the most fractious press atmospheres in living memory. He is a product of this as much as Elizabeth II was of her own sheltered, loving childhood.

Unsurprisingly, Charles never discussed his feelings on the role that awaited him in public and, considering the emotional ramifications of his accession, that is hardly surprising. When it comes to what sort of a constitutional monarch Charles will be, the jury is still out. Some commentators believe that Charles's entire life has been spent pushing the boundaries of the role that he was born to inherit. He has cultivated an inner circle of highly knowledgeable and influential experts in his fields of interest and has kept in regular touch with policymakers through meetings and sometimes controversial correspondence. During his time as Prince of Wales his lobbying on behalf of his interests had been seen by the public as proof of Charles's dedication to the causes that concern him, but as a constitutional monarch that may now change.

Firstly, there is the question of what is appropriate. Charles will undoubtedly be a different sort of monarch to his mother. He has been outspoken and unapologetic in his interests and might be unwilling to step back and adopt the neutral position that was favoured by his

A family duty

mother. In fact, having spent decades preparing to take on the role of monarch, it's questionable whether he would even want to simply mimic one of the most popular sovereigns that the country has ever known.

Charles is a man who has always been thoroughly unapologetic about his dedication to duty and who has, for better or worse, been honest when presenting himself in public. If he were to try and simply ape Queen Elizabeth II it would go against everything that Charles was at pains to demonstrate throughout his long years as Prince of Wales. Even so, he will now certainly have to give a great deal of thought and consideration to his lobbying activities. Every word will have to be weighed to ensure that it doesn't breach the boundaries of a constitutional head of state and to equally be certain that they are reflections of the new monarch's own beliefs, not his late mother's.

Charles, however, is a man of duty and intelligence. He will certainly not be out to cause any scandals or create anarchy but to ensure stability not only at home but across the world. His ties to the government and senior policymakers and experts might prove to be very useful, rather

REDUCING WORKING ROYALS
With the focus on the cost of the royal family ever unwavering, Charles is expected to take a scythe to the numbers of working royals

In the media storm surrounding Prince Andrew's BBC interview regarding his friendship with the convicted sex offender Jeffrey Epstein, the media spotlight swung once more onto what exactly the so-called working royals do to earn their pay. Having stepped down from his official duties supposedly at the behest of Charles, as Prince Andrew was removed from his role, long-whispered rumours regarding his older brother's plans for the future of the royal family suddenly became louder than ever.

If those rumours are to be believed, Charles supposedly plans to fire the vast majority of working royals early in his reign. It is a subject that has always been close to his heart but one that has only recently come to public knowledge in the furore surrounding the actions of his younger brother. It is believed that Charles intends to reduce the large selection of working royals down to a very select inner circle of immediate family consisting of himself and his wife, together with Prince William, his wife, and their children. In doing so, he will bring the British royal family further into line with their European counterparts, creating a far more streamlined and easy to control household.

than a cause for concern, and he certainly didn't operate in a vacuum in his role as Prince of Wales. Instead he spent decades building a highly supportive and long-standing team who are dedicated not only to offering Charles guidance and their own perspectives but also to discussing matters of public concern with him. Nobody understands better than Charles that the differences between the life and responsibilities of the Prince of Wales and the monarch are not to be underestimated, and nobody is better prepared to negotiate that change. Unlike many other former heirs to the throne, Charles was thoroughly and strictly prepared for his role, first at his mother's behest and then by his own responsibilities throughout his life.

Charles no doubt recognises that he might have to step back from day-to-day involvement in charitable and political lobbying. Quite apart from matters of constitutional concern, Charles's already full diary will now become even more packed, and as he grows older he will certainly find himself having to be more choosy and realistic about what he can expect of himself. His eldest son already has a pronounced public role, and it's likely that his role and responsibilities will increase for Prince William. As the next in line to the throne, William has also spent his life in preparation to one day be king, and though the title of Prince of Wales isn't a hereditary one, whether the new king bestows it on William or not, the prince will step into his father's shoes as the next king in waiting and probably take up many of the duties that his father has had to relinquish in order to focus on those of a monarch.

All those involved hope that the transition from the late Queen Elizabeth II to her heir will be a smooth one, but there are those who believe it will be a challenging time for Charles and the country despite the preparations that have been made. Given Charles's understandable reluctance to discuss the matter, all we can really go on is the man himself. He is in many ways unlike his mother, but in one thing they were always very alike indeed, and that is their heartfelt dedication to the duty that has been entrusted to them.

Though Charles spoke very little on the subject of succession prior to the Queen's passing, he has been entirely honest about his wish to continue the work he championed when Prince of Wales. Chief among the initiatives that he wants to carry forward into his reign is his desire to bring people together in a spirit of learning and sharing to focus on issues that impact everybody, from the environment to building communities. He has acknowledged that his personal approach as a lobbyist may now have to take a different form, but it's something he has heretofore demurred from discussing in detail. His critics sometimes argue that Charles is incapable of being a neutral constitutional monarch and that, having spent decades meddling - as some see it - in government business, being head of state will have little effect on his outspoken behaviour, particularly on issues he feels strongly about. Yet Charles has always acknowledged that a change of some magnitude will be necessary. How great a change that will be and what form his reign will take could have a profound impact on the future of the British monarchy. It is something that a man as intelligent, conscientious and dedicated as Charles will be keenly aware of as he sets out on the most important and unforgiving role of his life.

Even as a young man, Charles was confident in duties that included meeting figures such as US President Richard Nixon

A family duty

"CHARLES SPENT DECADES BUILDING A HIGHLY SUPPORTIVE TEAM WHO ARE DEDICATED TO OFFERING HIM GUIDANCE"

Following Hurricane Katrina, the royal couple visited New Orleans to meet victims of the hurricane and representatives of the emergency services

Charles III has been committed to saving the environment for decades

DEDICATED TO SUSTAINABILITY

From his youth, Charles has been committed to the care of the environment. Once derided as an eccentric, today his dedication has proven to be well-placed. Far from being bizarre or far-fetched, his views were way ahead of their time

Words **Catherine Curzon**

All his life, Charles III has felt a particular connection with the British countryside and the natural environment. Over the decades, that connection has turned into a dedication to conservation and the wellbeing of the planet. While some of his siblings became more well-known for their dedication to the glitzy high life and all the scandal that went with it, Charles was always happier seeking sanctuary in nature. Initially his passion for environmental matters attracted derision, with Charles mocked as the eccentric royal who talked to trees and believed they could listen, but over the decades he's been proven to be a man ahead of his time when it comes to issues of conservation concern.

In the early 1980s, Charles's interest in the natural environment began to become public knowledge. It was something that the famously reserved royal felt strongly about and a message that he believed he needed to share. In fact, perhaps he was a little too honest, as before long he had achieved notoriety as an eccentric prince who liked nothing more than a chat with the contents of his greenhouse. Yet Charles took the mockery on the chin, as well as cynical suggestions from some quarters that he had plenty of time to spend among the trees because he was usually away with the fairies. But he wasn't deterred. As the media flocked to cover every twist and turn of his first marriage, he retreated from the spotlight and focused on his environmental interests as a way to distract himself from the dramas at home.

In 1986 Charles converted the Duchy of Cornwall's Home Farm to organic practices. At the time this was a highly controversial move that was used by some as further evidence that the then heir to the throne was badly out of touch with the public. In big business and in major supermarkets the focus was on piling products high and selling them cheap, but at Duchy Home Farm, the prices might have increased but the products were guaranteed to be farmed organically and ethically. It was a move that attracted derision from shoppers who were feeling the pinch of recession, yet in fact the Duchy brand was at the vanguard of organic production. Today, there is a greater emphasis than ever on organic produce, which has become commonplace, and the same supermarkets who were held up as the ideal for their mass-produced, low-priced and intensively produced goods now offer extensive organic ranges of their own. Ironically, some of them stock Duchy products too.

Yet Charles wasn't content to be satisfied with organic farming and in the 1980s and 1990s he believed that his position as heir to the throne could be used to further his environmental concerns. Though members of the royal family are expected to remain politically neutral, Charles hit the headlines for the so-called Black Spider memos in which he wrote to senior British political figures to share his opinions on a variety of environmental issues ranging from climate change to sustainable farming and fisheries. Though the Prince of Wales certainly wasn't attempting to influence policy openly, he was certainly determined to draw the attention of policy makers to the minutiae of environmental concerns, lending a level of detail that it was possible they might otherwise have been unaware of.

Thanks to Charles's efforts to raise awareness, the government of the day was able to take far more educated decisions on occasionally obscure conservation issues. He never attempted to further his own interests either; his attentions were firmly focused on the planet. There was no suggestion that Charles would gain anything whatsoever from the memos, but the natural environment certainly did. At least partially thanks to Charles and his letters to Elliot Morley, at the time in office as the minister for the environment, the endangered albatross, which had seen its numbers devastated by discarded fishing boats and nets, was buoyed by an investment of tens of thousands of pounds in environmental clean-up efforts intended to halt its decline.

Once mocked, the Duchy Originals brand has become a household name

DUCHY ORIGINALS

The iconic Duchy Originals brand has been setting the organic standard for decades

Though Charles's Duchy Home Farm went organic as long ago as 1986, it wasn't until 1992 that he set up Duchy Originals, providing food and produce grown both on the farm itself and by suppliers who followed the same sustainable practices. Though derided as expensive and indulgent back in the early 1990s, as interest in organic and sustainable food flourished, the brand became a pioneer.

Of course, it hasn't been without its critics. Charles and Duchy Originals as a company faced derision for including homeopathic medicines in its product line, a discipline that Charles champions both personally and on his farm. Duchy Originals has also been criticised for having products manufactured by big businesses that don't necessarily follow organic methods, as well as for sourcing some items from overseas rather than farmers at home. Although Charles has answered his critics and explained why such decisions have occasionally been taken, it has led some to question whether Duchy Originals remains true to its ideals.

The healthy profits derived from the sale of Duchy Originals products are ploughed back into The Prince's Trust, a charity Charles founded. Duchy Originals continues to flourish, proving that what might have seemed like a pipe dream was anything but.

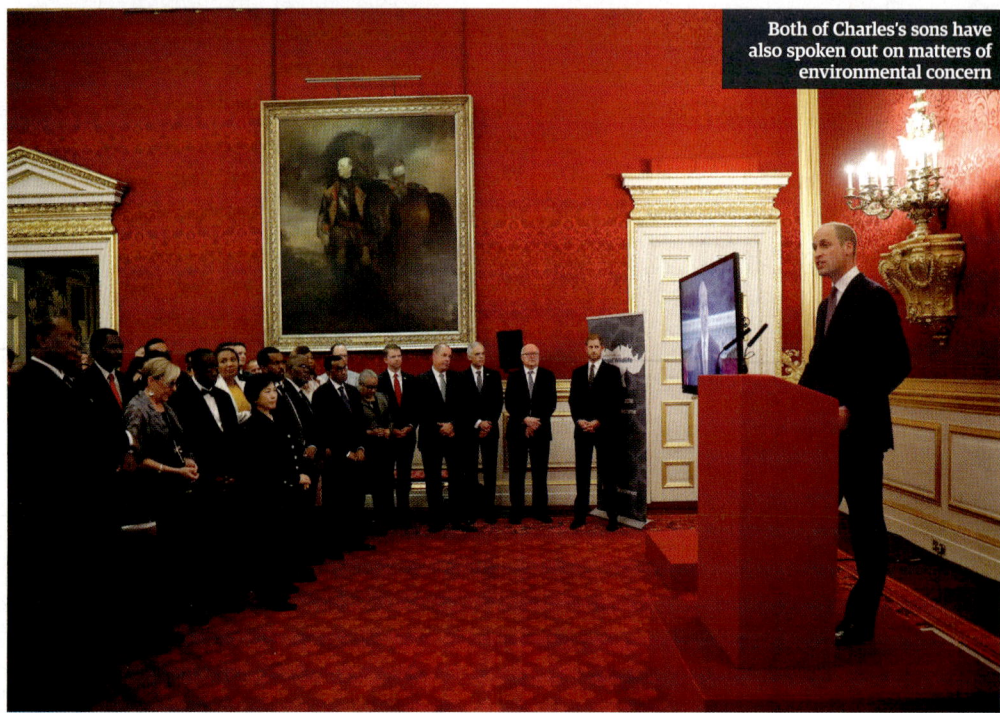

Both of Charles's sons have also spoken out on matters of environmental concern

Dedicated to sustainability

With a worldwide platform that far outstrips that of most other campaigners, Charles is uniquely placed to work for the initiatives he believes in. For four decades, long before his views became fashionable, he was attempting to educate the public on the importance of sustainability, from climate change to pollution. While eschewing pesticides and chemicals on his domestic estate, he also ensured that his own household has become a leader in environmental change. The household of the Prince of Wales made its emissions a matter of public record and did everything in its power to move from fossil fuels to sustainable energy sources, including solar panels at Charles's residences and other premises related to his businesses and activities. Where possible, biomass boilers heated the royal buildings, and where a sustainable alternative was available that's what Charles plumped for, from central heating to the light bulbs at Highgrove.

Even this most eco-friendly royal household, however, was not able to completely eradicate its carbon footprint. In order to address the imbalance, Charles invested in sustainable forestry and supported and donated to organisations that campaign against deforestation. When it comes to waste, Charles also become a pacesetter. His estates reused rainwater and other waste water, and his companies and households all subscribed to sustainability commitments ranging from composting food waste to replacing paper with electronic communications wherever possible and reusing and recycling paper when hard copies must be used. There is, however, one area in which the king is unshakeable. He completely opposes the installation of wind farms on the royal estates and has, in his outspoken fashion, described them as an ugly blot on the national landscape.

Charles III has always been a busy public figure who undertakes more travel than the vast majority of people. Though his environmental credentials at home are impeccable, when he's out and about they're equally trailblazing. It's impossible for Charles and his wife to avoid travelling, but they have set the example that their households are expected to follow. While issues such as logistics, cost and security are considered in great detail for royal travel, Charles added the carbon footprint of his duties to those considerations. The carbon impact of each and every official trip he made as Prince of Wales was monitored and recorded yearly from 2007 onwards to ensure that every measure possible to reduce it was taken, though this hasn't prevented critics from asking why Charles and other members of his immediate family have continued to travel by private jet. Charles's personal Aston Martin has been converted to run on bioethanol produced from a cocktail of cheese and wine by-products, which seems so perfectly Charles, and when on official business he travels in electric vehicles wherever possible while trying to ensure that any taxis his household requires are low-emission.

On the wider stage, Charles has been the driving force behind a number of international initiatives intended to promote his belief that economic development and social welfare are uniquely tied to nature and the promotion of environmental concerns. It was a message he shared with the nation in 1990 via his documentary film, *The Earth in Balance*, which was shown

Charles visited the Somerset Levels to lend his support to victims of flooding in 2014

At Highgrove House, Charles has practised sustainability both inside and out

on the BBC. In this film he attempted to overcome his distant and formal image by making a personal plea for humanity to reconsider its relationship with the natural environment. He travelled the globe to look at not only the issues facing the planet but to learn more about what could be done to combat them. It was a film unlike any made by a member of the royal family before.

In 2019 he appeared on ITV in a two-part documentary, *Prince Charles: Inside the Duchy of Cornwall*, in which he showcased the talents of the farmers and tenants on Duchy land. Above all things, he admitted, he was terrified that the hard work being done by the farmers might be undone by global warming and climate change, which the world at large must take seriously and do everything to fight against.

In addition to his work on film, Charles has written books and articles on matters of environmental concern. In the gift shop at Highgrove a handpicked selection of books encouraging organic farming fly off the shelves in ever-growing numbers, reflecting the widespread interest in limiting the use of chemicals on the land. Yet while he is an educator, the king also remains a keen student even in his senior years. He has undertaken innumerable fact-finding meetings with farmers, scientists and other interested parties around the world and has encouraged networking between different groups, including the Prince's May Day Network, which encourages business leaders to make proactive moves to combat climate change. His influence has always proved useful when it came to facilitating the exchange of expertise for the benefit of Earth.

Charles has not been without laurels in recognition of his efforts either. He has received the Global Environmental Citizen Award and spoken to governments and world leaders including former US President Donald Trump, who has never been noted for his own belief in climate change. Yet Charles doesn't only mix with illustrious names, and when the Somerset levels flooded, leaving people homeless and businesses ruined, he visited them to make a pledge of funding in order to help those who had lost so much.

Charles believes that nothing is so threatening to the future of the planet as climate change and he continues to campaign for governments and citizens alike to play their part in turning back the tide. Whether encouraging his household staff to follow his conservation examples or undertaking charitable initiatives on a vast scale, he has learned to tailor his work to his audience. In 2017 he penned the introduction to a series of Ladybird books for adults aimed at discussing scientific issues in an accessible manner and providing real-world examples of simple changes that readers can make to do their bit. Frustrated with misinformation and misunderstanding, Charles's voice on the matter of the environment has never been louder than it is in the 21st century, at what he believes is the point of no return. In a world where politicians are not always held to account for missing targets, Charles has been calling them out.

Charles's own sons have spoken of their pride at their father's works and have followed in his conservationist speeches. Prince Harry, whose relationship with Charles has sometimes been fractious, gave a speech to the Australian Geographic Awards in which he talked about how much he respected Charles for never giving up on his efforts to educate the world on environmental matters, even when the world didn't want to listen.

Charles has been committed to saving the environment for decades

THE CARBUNCLE SPEECH

Charles doesn't only campaign for the natural world; he has plenty to say about the built environment too

Charles III has never shied away from making known his feelings on the built environment. In 1984 the man behind the model village of Poundbury, which takes inspiration from traditional architectural styles, gave a speech in which he condemned a planned extension to the National Gallery as a "monstrous carbuncle", arguing that it was entirely inappropriate and ill-suited to the architecture surrounding it. To Charles, harmony in the built environment was as important as harmony in the natural world and in the proposed extension, designed by Ahrends Burton Koralek, Charles saw nothing but disharmony writ large.

In his controversial speech, Charles asked whether architects and planners ever listened to the opinion of the man in the street, who would have to live with the building every day. Innovation and modernism for the sake of it cut no ice with him; instead he believed that architects should focus on the reality of day-to-day living and look at ways in which buildings could create and nurture a community, providing an environment that is conducive to modern living and comfort.

With the overwhelming support of the public, Charles got his way. The 'monstrous carbuncle' remained a proposal, never to rise above London.

Prince William, meanwhile, began 2020 with the announcement of a new multi-million pound prize to help environmental visionaries battle the environmental issues that plague the planet. For a man who has long worked to ensure that the next generation of adults continue the work he has started, to see his sons take up the baton must have been a proud and touching moment for Charles.

Though he has never been at the forefront of fashion, when it came to the environmental impact of the catwalk, Charles set the trend yet again. In summer 2019 he entered a collaboration with the British fashion house Vin and Omi to produce clothes made out of nettles harvested from the Highgrove estate. Once a waste product, now the nettles were part of a bigger movement, with the collaboration attracting high-profile headlines and supporters across the world.

The so-called eccentric who was once ridiculed for talking to trees and championing organic farming has long since become a familiar and authoritative face at the highest-profile environmental summits. Despite his reputation for being an old-fashioned pillar of the establishment, the king recognises the importance of empowering the worlds' youth to take action. Yet though he places the onus for the future of the planet on the generations that will inherit it, he hasn't let the groups who contributed to climate change, deforestation and environmental catastrophe walk away from the issue. Instead he has called on world leaders to provide resources to empower future generations to continue to work in the interests of the planet and all who share it.

From the International Sustainability Unit to community initiatives across the nation, Charles has been at pains to help people understand that every little helps. He is the patron of many environmental charities and in 2017 was the recipient of the prestigious GCC Global Leader of Change Award, which recognised his dedication to the preservation of the environment for the sake of humanity's future. His passion, dedication and depth of knowledge have made Charles III an authoritative and respected figure across the globe. His passion and relentless advocacy for the future of the world and its food sources is admirable. In the work he has done for the wellbeing of the natural world and those who will inherit it, he has proven his mettle time and again.

A sombre King Charles III stands on guard beside his late mother's coffin, accompanied by his siblings

LONG LIVE THE KING

When King Charles III succeeded to the throne, his life changed forever

Words Catherine Curzon & Jessica Leggett

Late in the afternoon on 8 September 2022, Queen Elizabeth II died at Balmoral Castle. By the time of her death, hours before the public were aware that she had passed away, Operation London Bridge was already in action. Operation London Bridge was the code name given to the formal funeral and mourning plans for Her late Majesty, and the queen herself had played her part in devising it. The plan, which was revisited and revised three times a year, covered the announcement of the monarch's death, the period of official mourning required and the most minute details of her state funeral. That funeral took place at Westminster Abbey on 19 September, after four days in which the queen lay in state at Westminster Hall.

As the late queen's coffin began its final journey from Balmoral to London, her eldest son, King Charles III, began his monarchical duties. He was at his mother's bedside in the final hours of her life and succeeded to the throne at the moment of her passing. King Charles III spent the evening of his mother's death at Balmoral with Camilla, Queen Consort, before the couple travelled to Buckingham Palace together the following day. Upon their arrival, the visibly emotional couple spent time meeting members of the public who had gathered to mourn the late queen and offer their commiserations to their new sovereign.

That afternoon, King Charles was occupied with his first meeting with Prime Minister Liz Truss, before he made his first address to the nation as king. In it, he paid heartfelt tribute to the late

queen as both a mother and monarch and thanked the public for their warm regards and kind words. With a promise to pledge himself to the duty and service of the crown, the new king prepared himself for a week of ceremony.

On the morning of 10 September, the Accession Council met in the throne room of St James's Palace and there proclaimed Charles king. As the world watched, he pledged himself to his new duty and signed his signature, Charles R, on two copies of the Scottish Oath. He then returned to Buckingham Palace to greet the crowds gathered there once more.

That afternoon, the king met with the prime minster again before attending several meetings with members of the Cabinet and the leaders of opposition parties.

As the new week began, the king and queen consort attended a ceremony in the historic Westminster Hall, where they received expressions of condolence from the House of Commons and the House of Lords. From there, they embarked on a tour of the United Kingdom that took them to the Palace of Holyroodhouse in Edinburgh, where the king participated in the Ceremony of the Keys. He then joined his siblings for a procession along the Royal Mile, following the hearse conveying his mother towards St Giles' Cathedral.

As huge queues began to form to view the coffin as it lay in state, King Charles III attended an audience with Nicola Sturgeon, Scotland's First Minister, before he received a Motion of Condolence from the Scottish Parliament. He then returned to the cathedral to join his siblings in what was only the third Vigil of the Princes in history. As the public filed past the coffin, the king, the Princess Royal, the Duke of York and the Earl of Wessex stood silent guard around their mother's coffin for ten minutes.

While the coffin of Her late Majesty began its journey to London on 13 September, King Charles III and Camilla, Queen Consort, travelled to Belfast, Northern Ireland, where crowds had gathered to welcome the royal visitors. The king and queen consort attended an exhibition at Hillsborough Castle before Charles undertook meetings with the Secretary of State for Northern Ireland and Irish party leaders. He then received condolences from the Speaker of the Northern Ireland Assembly and attended a reception. It was then time to travel to St Anne's Cathedral for a service.

A week after his accession, King Charles III joined members of the royal family to accompany his late mother's coffin from Buckingham Palace to Westminster Hall as part of the formal funeral cortege. The royal family then attended a short service to mark the beginning of the period in which the coffin of Queen Elizabeth II would lay in state before the king was on the road again. He and Camilla concluded the week and his tour of the four nations with a visit to Wales on Friday. Once again, he attended a service of prayer and met political leaders, as well as spending time meeting the people who had gathered to see him and the queen consort.

The funeral of Queen Elizabeth II took place on 19 September, a national holiday in the United Kingdom. King Charles III led his family as they processed behind the coffin of Her late Majesty from Westminster Hall to Westminster Abbey, where the funeral service began. At its conclusion, the queen's coffin and the royal family travelled on to Windsor, where Elizabeth II was laid to rest in St George's Chapel.

While the national mourning period lasted ten days, ending on the day of the queen's funeral, Charles announced that royal mourning would be extended by a further seven days. This extra time allowed the king, his family, and the royal household to grieve privately for the loss of the queen after being under a period of extreme pressure, with their grief broadcast to the world. Following the funeral, Charles and Camilla went to their Birkhall home, on the Balmoral Estate, to grieve in peace.

Following the end of the royal mourning period, Buckingham Palace released a new photograph of Charles and Camilla, with William and Catherine, the new Prince and Princess of Wales. The photo, taken on 18 September, the day before the queen's funeral, shows the four smiling and dressed in all black for mourning. For many, the photo represented a glimpse of the streamlined monarchy that Charles is reportedly keen to achieve.

The king arrives at St Giles' Cathedral alongside sister, Princess Anne, Prince Andrew and Prince Edward (not pictured)

Long live the king

Sporting the Imperial State Crown, Orb and Sceptre, the queen's coffin is borne out of the abbey

This photo of Camilla and Charles, with the Prince and Princess of Wales, was taken the day before the queen's state funeral

The king and queen consort during their visit to Dunfermline, Scotland

King Charles has vowed to honour his duty to his country and to his late mother

King Charles meets Rishi Sunak, his new prime minister, following the resignation of Liz Truss

With royal mourning over, Charles and Camilla travelled to Dunfermline in Scotland, on 3 October, to celebrate its new city status, which was awarded during the late queen's Platinum Jubilee. The visit was personal for the king and, in his speech, he stated that his mother's "deep love for Scotland was one of the foundations of her life."

Charles had only been king for six weeks when he was confronted with Liz Truss's resignation as prime minister on 20 October. Appointed just three days before the queen's death, Truss resigned after losing the confidence of her party, largely caused by a disastrous mini-budget that led to financial instability for the UK. Rishi Sunak was the sole nominee in the subsequent leadership contest and was invited by the king to form a government, becoming the first prime minister to be appointed during Charles's reign.

After a quiet few weeks, the Duke and Duchess of Sussex's Netflix documentary, Harry & Meghan, refocused attention on the king and the royal family in December. The documentary explored the couple's relationship from its beginning to their decision to step back as working royals, their relocation to California and their life together since.

The widely anticipated series quickly became Netflix's second most successful documentary series, breaking the record for the streaming service's biggest debut. The series - recorded before the queen's death - received mixed reviews, and both Buckingham Palace and Kensington Palace declined to comment. The couple were highly critical of the British tabloid press and the racist undertones in the way Meghan was reported on, and they also claimed that Palace officials would leak stories to the media. Although it was not a flattering portrayal of royal life, the documentary did not reveal a lot of new information, prompting many to speculate that Charles and the rest of the royal family would be relieved.

Prince Harry's eagerly awaited autobiography, Spare, reveals many of his grievances

Of course, a little more than a week after the series ended, focus shifted to Charles's first Christmas message, which was recorded in St George's Chapel at Windsor Castle. In addition to paying tribute to his mother, the king reflected on a variety of topics, including the importance of faith, the dedication of those in public service, and community spirit. The king's first Christmas message set a new record for the most watched Christmas TV address by a monarch.

With the success of the king's Christmas message still fresh, it wasn't long before a media frenzy was whipped up again with the release of Prince Harry's autobiography, Spare, in January 2023. In comparison to the Netflix documentary, the duke's highly personal and revealing autobiography laid bare many of his grievances with his family, most notably his conflict with his brother William, as well as his continued grief at the loss of his mother, Diana, Princess of Wales. Spare released a lot of previously unknown information about the royals into the public domain, but again, Buckingham Palace and Kensington Palace refused to comment.

It is hardly surprising that after the recent revelations made by the Duke and Duchess of Sussex, it has been questioned whether the couple will be present for Charles's coronation. It is believed that with the current cost-of-living crisis in the UK, the king is keen to slim down the

Long live the king

The king's first Christmas message was a ratings success

coronation, and non-working royals have never had an official place in the ceremony. While we don't know what decision will be made, the debate over their attendance is sure to feature in the media and behind closed doors for the next few months.

What we do know, however, is that Charles's coronation will take place on 6 May 2023 at Westminster Abbey. Much has changed in the seven decades since Queen Elizabeth II was crowned, and the ceremony is reportedly going to change to reflect that the United Kingdom is a multicultural and multi-faith country today.

As king, Charles III has stated his intention to honour his duty to his country. The longest-serving heir apparent in British history, he was an outspoken Prince of Wales, known for championing many causes dear to his heart. Although he will no longer be able to campaign in the same way, he is expected to continue his patronage of the arts as well as his dedication to issues such as the environment and agricultural matters.

Most of all, Charles will seek to be a monarch who unifies his kingdom, offering stability and continuity in the wake of his mother's death. He is a man of traditions but one prepared to modernise, and he understands the importance of keeping the monarchy relevant. With the support of both his family and the public, King Charles III will steer the monarchy into the future.

The king is said to want to promote the UK's diversity and multiculturalism during his coronation

> I AM DEEPLY AWARE OF THIS GREAT INHERITANCE AND OF THE DUTIES AND HEAVY RESPONSIBILITIES OF SOVEREIGNTY WHICH HAVE NOW PASSED TO ME... I SHALL STRIVE TO FOLLOW THE INSPIRING EXAMPLE I HAVE BEEN SET...